AA E

Latin A

Spanish

phrase book

AA Publishing

Contents

Is it going to snow?	¿Va a nevar? *bah ah nehbahr?*
Is it going to freeze?	¿Va a helar? *bah ah ehlahr?*
Is the thaw setting in?	¿Comenzará el deshielo? *kohmehnsahrah ehl dehsyehloh*
Is it going to be foggy?	¿Habrá niebla? *ahbrah nyehblah?*
Is there going to be a thunderstorm?	¿Habrá tormenta eléctrica? *ahbrah tohrmehntah ehlehktreekah?*
The weather's changing	Va a cambiar el tiempo *bah ah kahmbyahr ehl tyehmpoh*
It's cooling down	Va a refrescar *bah ah rehfrehskahr*
What's the weather going to be like today/ tomorrow?	¿Qué tiempo hará hoy/mañana? *keh tyehmpoh ahrah oy/mahnyahnah?*

algo nublado/nublado
light/heavy clouds
bochornoso
stormy
bueno
fine
caluroso
hot
chubasco
shower
cielo cubierto
overcast
desapacible
bleak
despejado
clear
escarcha
frost
fresco
chilly
frío
cold
granizo
hail
...grados (bajo/sobre cero)
...degrees (above/ below zero)
helada
(black) ice
húmedo
damp
huracán
hurricane
llovizna
drizzle
lluvia
rain
lluvioso
wet
niebla
fog
nieve
snow
nublado
cloudy
ola de calor
heat wave
pesado
muggy
sofocante
scorching hot
soleado
sunny
suave
mild
tormenta eléctrica
thunderstorm
vendaval
gale
ventoso
windy
viento
wind
viento leve /moderado/ fuerte
light/moderate/ strong wind
tempestad
squall

1.6 Here, there...

See also 5.1 Asking for directions

here/there	aquí/allá *ahkee/ahlyah*
somewhere/nowhere	en alguna/ninguna parte *ehn algoonah/neengoonah pahrteh*
everywhere	en todas partes *ehn tohdahs pahrtehs*
far away/nearby	lejos/cerca *lehhos/sehrkah*
right/left	a la derecha/izquierda *ah lah dehrehchah/eeskyehrdah*

to the right/left of	a la derecha/izquierda de	*ah lah dehrehchah/eeskyehrdah deh*
straight ahead	todo recto	*tohdoh rehktoh*
via	pasando por	*pahsahndoh pohr*
in	en	*ehn*
on	sobre	*sohbreh*
under	debajo de	*dehbahhoh deh*
against	contra	*kohntrah*
opposite	frente a	*frehnteh ah*
next to	al lado de	*ahl lahdoh deh*
near	junto a	*hoontoh ah*
in front of	delante de	*dehlahnteh deh*
in the centre	en el medio	*ehn ehl mehdyoh*
forward	hacia adelante	*ahsyah ahdehlanteh*
down	(hacia) abajo	*(ahsyah) ahbahhoh*
up	(hacia) arriba	*(ahsya) ahrreebah*
inside	(hacia) adentro	*(ahsya) ahdehntroh*
outside	(hacia) afuera	*(ahsya) ahfwehrah*
behind	(hacia) atrás	*(ahsya) ahtrahs*
at the front	delante	*dehlahnteh*
at the back	detrás	*dehtrahs*
in the north	en el norte	*ehn ehl nohrteh*
to the south	hacia el sur	*ahsya ehl soor*
from the west	del oeste	*dehl ohehsteh*
from the east	del este	*dehl ehsteh*
...of	al...de	*ahl...deh*

1.7 What does that sign say?

See 5.4 Traffic signs

abierto/cerrado
open/closed
agua no potable
no drinking water
alta tensión
high voltage
elevador
lift
caballeros
gents/gentlemen
caja
pay here
completo
full
propiedad privada
private (property)
cuidado con el perro
beware of the dog
cuidado, escalón
mind the step
entrada
entrance
entrada libre
free admission
escalera
stairs
escalera de incendios
fire escape
escalera mecánica
escalator
freno de emergencia
emergency brake
horario (de apertura)
opening hours
información
information
liquidación (por cese)
closing-down sale
no funciona
out of order
no tocar
please do not touch
peligro
danger
peligro de incendio
fire hazard
...piso
...floor
primeros auxilios
first aid
prohibido el paso
no entry
prohibido fotografiar
no photographs
prohibido fumar
no smoking
prohibido hacer fuego
no open fires
prohibido para animales
no pets allowed
prohibido pisar el césped
keep off the grass
información
inquiries
rebajas
clearance
recepción
reception
recién pintado
wet paint
reservado
reserved
saldos
sale
salida
exit
salida de emergencia/salida de socorro
emergency exit
se alquila
for hire
se ruega no molestar
do not disturb
se vende
for sale
damas
ladies
baños
toilets
empujar/jalar (tirar)
push/pull

1.8 Telephone alphabet

Pronouncing the alphabet, e.g. A as in Ana

a	*ah*	de Ana	*deh ahnah*
b	*beh*	de bueno	*deh bwehnoh*
c	*seh*	de Carlos	*deh kahrlohs*
ch	*cheh*	de chocolate	*deh choh kohlahteh*
d	*deh*	de dedo	*deh dehdoh*
e	*eh*	de Eduardo	*deh ehdwahrdoh*
f	*hefeh*	de Francia	*deh frahnthyah*
g	*heh*	de gato	*deh gahtoh*
h	*ahcheh*	de historia	*de eestohryah*
I	*ee*	de Inés	*deh eenehs*
j	*hohtah*	de José	*deh hohseh*
k	*kah*	de Kilo	*deh keeloh*

l	ehleh	de Luis	deh lwees
ll	ehlyeh	de Llanes	deh lyahnehs
m	ehmeh	de Madrid	deh Mahdreedh
n	ehneh	de Norma	deh nohrmah
ñ	ehnyeh	de ñoño	deh nyohnyoh
o	oh	de Omar	deh ohmahr
p	peh	de Pedro	deh pehdroh
q	koo	de querido	deh kehreedoh
r	ehrreh	de Ramón	deh rahmohn
s	ehseh	de sábado	deh sahbahdoh
t	teh	de Teresa	deh tehrehsah
u	oo	de Ulises	deh ooleesehs
v	beh	de Victor	deh beektohr
w	dohblehbeh	de Washington	deh washeengtohn
x	ehkees	de Xiquena	deh heekehnah
y	ee	griega	gryehgah
z	thehtah	de Zaragoza	deh thahrahgohthah

1.9 Personal details

surname	apellido *ahpehlyeedoh*
christian name(s)	nombre *nohmbreh*
initials	iniciales *eeneeyahlehs*
address (street/number)	dirección (calle/número) *deerehksyohn (kahlyeh/noomehroh)*
post code/town	código postal/población *cohdeegoh pohstahl/pohblahsyon)*
sex (male/female)	sexo (v = varón, m = mujer) *sehksoh (v = bahrohn, m = moohehr)*
nationality	nacionalidad *nahsyohnahleedah*
date of birth	fecha de nacimiento *fehchah deh nahseemyehntoh*
place of birth	lugar de nacimiento *loogahr deh naseemyehntoh*
occupation	profesión *profehsyohn*
married/single/divorced	casado, casada/soltero, soltera/ divorciado, divorciada *kahsahdoh, kahsahdah/sohltehroh, sohltehrah/deebohrsyahdoh, deebohrsyahdah*
widowed	viuda/viudo *byoodah/byoodoh*
(number of) children	(número de) hijos *(noomehroh deh) eehohs*
passport/identity card/driving licence/ number, place and date of issue	pasaporte/carnet de identidad/permiso de conducir/número, lugar y fecha de expedición *pahsahpohrteh/kahrneh deh eedehnteedahdh/pehrmeesoh deh kohndooseer/noomehroh, loogahr ee fehchah deh ehkspehdeesyohn*

2

Courtesies

2 Courtesies

- **Female friends and relatives** kiss on one cheek in Latin American countries. In shops, etc., you will hear *¡Buenos días!* or just *¡Buenas!*

2.1 Greetings

Hello	Hola, buenos días *ohlah, bwehnohs deeahs*
Hello, Peter	Hola, Pedro *ohlah, pehdroh*
Hi, Helen	Qué tal, Elena *keh tahl, ehlehnah*
Good morning, madam	Buenos días, señora (before midday) *bwehnohs deeahs, sehnyohrah*
Good afternoon, sir	Buenas tardes, señor (after midday) *bwehnahs tahrdehs, sehnyohr*
Good evening	Buenas tardes (before 7pm), buenas noches (after 7pm) *bwehnahs tahrdehs, bwehnahs nohchehs*
How are you?	¿Qué tal? *keh tahl?*
Fine, thank you, and you?	Muy bien, ¿y usted? *mwee byehn, ee oostehdh?*
Very well	Estupendo *ehstoopehndoh*
Not very well	Regular *rehgoolahr*
Not too bad	Tirando *teerando*
I'd better be going	Bueno, me voy *bwehnoh, meh boy*
I have to be going. Someone's waiting for me	Tengo que irme. Me están esperando *tehngoh keh eermeh, meh ehstahn ehspehrahndoh*
Bye!	¡Adiós! *ahdyohs!*
Goodbye	Hasta luego *ahstah lwehgoh*
See you soon	Hasta pronto *ahstah prohntoh*
See you later	Hasta luego *ahstah lwehgoh*
See you in a little while	Hasta ahora *ahstah ahohrah*
Sleep well	Que descanse *keh dehskahnseh*
Good night	Buenas noches *bwehnahs nohchehs*
All the best	Que le vaya bien *keh leh bahyah byehn*
Have fun	Que se divierta, que lo pase bien *keh seh deebyehrtah, keh loh pahseh byehn*
Good luck	Mucha suerte *moochah swehrteh*

Have a nice holiday	Felices vacaciones *fehleesehs bahkahsyohnehs*
Have a good trip	Buen viaje *bwehn byahheh*
Thank you, you too	Gracias, igualmente *grahsyahs, eegwahlmehnteh*
Say hello to...for me	Saludos a... *sahloodohs ah...*
Who?	¿Quién? *kyehn?*

2.2 How to ask a question

Who's that?	¿Quién es? *kyehn ehs?*
What?	¿Qué? *keh?*
What's there to see here?	¿Qué se puede visitar aquí? *keh seh pwehdeh beeseetahr ahkee?*
What kind of hotel is that?	¿Qué clase de hotel es? *keh klahseh deh ohtehl ehs?*
Where?	¿Dónde? *dohndeh?*
Where's the toilet?	¿Dónde están los baños? *dohndeh ehstahn lohs bahnyohs?*
Where are you going?	¿A dónde va? *ahdohndeh bah?*
Where are you from?	¿De dónde es usted? *deh dohndeh ehs oostehdh?*
How?	¿Cómo? *kohmoh?*
How far is that?	¿A qué distancia queda? *ah keh deestahnsyah kehdah?*
How long does it take?	¿Cuánto dura? *kwahntoh doorah?*
How long is the trip?	¿Cuánto dura el viaje? *kwahntoh doorah ehl byahheh?*
How much?	¿Cuánto? *kwahntoh?*
How much is this?	¿Cuánto vale? *kwahntoh bahleh?*
What time is it?	¿Qué hora es? *keh ohrah ehs?*
Which?	¿Cuál? ¿Cuáles? *kwahl? kwahlehs?*
Which glass is mine?	¿Cuál es mi copa? *kwahl ehs mee kohpah?*
When?	¿Cuándo? *kwahndoh?*
When are you leaving?	¿Cuándo se va? *kwahndoh seh bah?*
Why?	¿Por qué? *pohr keh?*
Could you...me?	¿Podría...? *pohdreeah...?*
Could you help me, please?	¿Podría ayudarme? *pohdreeah ahyoodahrmeh?*

Could you point that out to me?	¿Me lo podría indicar? *meh loh pohdreeah eendeekahr?*
Could you come with me, please?	¿Puede acompañarme? *pwehdeh ahkohmpahnyahrmeh?*
Could you...	¿Quiere...?/¿Podría...? *kyehreh...?/pohdreeah...?*
Could you reserve some tickets for me, please?	¿Me podría reservar entradas? *meh pohdreeah rehsehrbahr ehntrahdahs?*
Do you know...?	¿Sabe...? *sahbeh...?*
Do you know another hotel, please?	¿Sabría indicarme otro hotel? *sahbreeah eendeekahrmeh ohtroh ohtehl?*
Do you know whether...?	¿Sabe si...? *sahbeh see...?*
Do you have a...?	¿Me podría dar un(a)...? *meh pohdreeah dahr oon(ah)...?*
Do you have a vegetarian dish, please?	¿Tendría comida vegetariana? *tehndreeah kohmeedah behhehtahreeahnah?*
I'd like...	Quisiera... *keesyehrah...*
I'd like a kilo of apples, please.	Quisiera un kilo de manzanas *keesyehrah oon keeloh deh mahnsahnahs*
Can I...?	¿Puedo...?/¿Se puede...? *pwehdoh...?/seh pwehdeh?*
Can I take this?	¿Podría llevármelo? *pohdreeah lyehbahrmehloh?*
Can I smoke here?	¿Se puede fumar aquí? *seh pwehdeh foomahr ahkee?*
Could I ask you something?	¿Puedo hacerle una pregunta? *pwehdoh ahsehrleh oonah prehgoontah?*

2.3 How to reply

Yes, of course	Sí, claro *see, klahroh*
No, I'm sorry	No, disculpe *noh, deeskoolpeh*
Yes, what can I do for you?	Sí. ¿En qué puedo servirle? *see, ehn keh pwehdoh sehrbeerleh?*
Just a moment, please	Un momento, por favor *oon mohmehntoh, pohr fahbohr*
No, I don't have time now	No, ahora no tengo tiempo *noh, aohrah noh tehngoh tyehmpoh*
No, that's impossible	No, eso es imposible *noh, ehsoh ehs eempohseebleh*
I think so	Creo que sí *krehoh keh see*
I agree	Estoy de acuerdo *ehstohee deh ahkwerdo*
I hope so too	Yo también lo espero *yoh tahmbyehn loh ehspehroh*
No, not at all	No, de ninguna manera *noh, deh neengoonah mahnehrah*
No, no-one	No, nadie *noh, nahdyeh*
No, nothing	No, nada *noh, nahdah*

That's (not) right	(No) es cierto	*(noh) ehs syehrtoh*
I (don't) agree	(No) estoy de acuerdo con usted	*(noh) ehstoy deh ahkwehrdoh kohn oostehdh*
All right	Está bien	*ehstah byehn*
Okay	De acuerdo	*deh ahkwehrdoh*
Perhaps	Quizá	*keesah*
I don't know	No lo sé	*noh loh seh*

2.4 Thank you

Thank you	Gracias	*grahsyahs*
You're welcome	De nada	*deh nahdah*
Thank you very much	Muchísimas gracias	*moocheeseemahs grahsyahs*
Very kind of you	Muy amable (de su parte)	*mwee ahmahbleh (deh soo pahrteh)*
I enjoyed it very much	Ha sido un verdadero placer	*ah seedoh oon behrdahdehroh plahsehr*
Thank you for your trouble	Gracias por la molestia	*grahsyahs pohr lah mohlehstyah*
You shouldn't have	No se hubiera molestado	*noh seh oobyehrah mohlehstahdoh*
That's all right	No se preocupe	*noh seh prehohkoopeh*

2.5 Sorry

Excuse me	Disculpe	*deeskoolpeh*
Sorry!	¡Perdón!	*pehrdohn!*
I'm sorry, I didn't know...	Perdón, no sabía que...	*pehrdohn, noh sahbeeah keh...*
I do apologise	Discúlpeme	*deeskoolpehmeh*
I'm sorry	Lo siento	*loh syehntoh*
I didn't do it on purpose, it was an accident	No lo hice a propósito; fue sin querer	*noh loh eeseh ah prohpohseetoh; fweh seen kehrehr*
That's all right	No importa	*noh eempohrtah*
Never mind	Déjelo	*dehhehloh*
It could've happened to anyone	Le puede pasar a cualquiera	*leh pwehdeh pahsahr ah kwahlkyehrah*
Which do you prefer?	¿Qué prefiere?	*keh prehfyehreh?*

2.6 What do you think?

What do you think?	¿Qué te parece? *keh teh pahrehseh?*
Don't you like dancing?	¿No te gusta bailar? *noh teh goostah bahylahr?*
I don't mind	Me da igual *meh dah eegwahl*
Well done!	¡Muy bien! *mwee byehn!*
Not bad!	¡No está mal! *noh ehstah mahl!*
Great!	¡Excelente! *ehksehlehnteh!*
Wonderful!	¡Qué delicia! *keh dehleesyah!*
It's really nice here!	¡Qué bien se está aquí! *keh byehn seh ehstah ahkee!*
How nice!	¡Qué lindo/bonito! *keh leendoh/bohneetoh!*
How nice for you!	¡Cuánto me alegro por usted! *kwahntoh meh ahlehgroh pohr oostehdh!*
I'm (not) very happy with...	(No) estoy muy contento con... *(noh) ehstoy mwee kohntehntoh kohn...*
I'm glad...	Me alegro de que... *meh ahlehgroh deh keh...*
I'm having a great time	Me estoy divirtiendo mucho *meh ehstoy deebeertyehndoh moochoh*
I'm looking forward to it	Tengo muchas ganas de... *tehngoh moochahs gahnahs deh...*
I hope it'll work out	Espero que salga bien *ehspehroh keh sahlgah byehn*
That's ridiculous!	¡Qué ridículo! *keh reedeekooloh!*
That's terrible!	¡Qué horror! *keh ohrrohr!*
What a pity!	¡Qué lástima! *keh lahsteemah!*
That's filthy!	¡Qué asco! *keh ahskoh!*
What a load of rubbish!	¡Qué tontería! *keh tohntehreeah!*
I don't like...	No me gusta... *noh meh goostah...*
I'm bored to death	Estoy muy aburrido *ehstoy mwee ahboorreedoh*
I've had enough	Estoy harto(a) *ehstoy ahrtoh(ah)*
This is no good	No puede ser *noh pwehdeh sehr*
I was expecting something completely different	Yo había esperado otra cosa *yoh ahbeeah ehspehrahdoh ohtrah kohsah*

3

Conversation

3 Conversation

3.1 I beg your pardon?

I don't speak any/ I speak a little...	No hablo/hablo un poco de... *noh ahbloh/ahbloh oon pohkoh deh...*
I'm English	Soy inglés/inglesa *soy eenglehs/eenglehsah*
I'm Scottish	Soy escocés/escocesa *soy ehskohsehs/ehskosehsah*
I'm Irish	Soy irlandés/irlandesa *soy eerlahndehs/eerlahndehsah*
I'm Welsh	soy galés/galesa *soy gahlehs/gahlehsah*
Do you speak English/French/German?	¿Habla inglés/francés/alemán? *ahblah eenglehs/frahnsehs/ahlehmahn?*
Is there anyone who speaks...?	¿Hay alguien que hable...? *ay ahlguyehn keh ahbleh...?*
I beg your pardon?	¿Cómo dice? *kohmoh deeseh?*
I (don't) understand	(No) entiendo *(noh) ehntyehndoh*
Do you understand me?	¿Me entiende? *meh ehntyehndeh?*
Could you repeat that, please?	¿Me lo podría repetir? *meh loh pohdreeah rehpehteer?*
Could you speak more slowly, please?	¿Podría hablar más despacio? *pohdreeah ahblahr mahs dehspahsyo?*
What does that (word) mean?	¿Qué significa esto/esta palabra? *keh seegneefeekah ehstoh/ehstah pahlahbrah?*
Is that similar to/the same as...?	¿Es (más o menos) lo mismo que...? *ehs mahs oh mehnohs loh meesmoh keh...?*
Could you write that down for me, please?	¿Podría escribírmelo? *pohdreeah eskreebeermehloh?*
Could you spell that for me, please?	¿Podría deletreármelo? *pohdreeah dehlehtrehahrmehloh?*

(See 1.8 Telephone alphabet)

Could you point that out in this phrase book, please?	¿Me lo podría señalar en esta guía? *meh loh pohdreeah sehnyahlahr ehn ehstah geeah?*
One moment, please, I have to look it up	Espere que lo busco en la guía *ehspehreh keh loh booskoh ehn lah geeah*
I can't find the word/the sentence	No puedo encontrar la palabra/la frase *noh pwehdoh ehnkohntrahr lah pahlahbrah/lah frahseh*
How do you say that in...?	¿Cómo se dice eso en...? *kohmoh seh deeseh ehstoh ehn...?*
How do you pronounce that?	¿Cómo se pronuncia? *kohmoh seh prohnoonsyah?*

3.2 Introductions

May I introduce myself?	Permítame presentarme	*pehrmeetahmeh prehsehntahrmeh*
My name's...	Me llamo...	*meh lyahmoh...*
I'm...	Soy...	*soy...*
What's your name?	¿Cómo se llama?	*kohmoh seh lyahmah?*
May I introduce...?	Permítame presentarle a...	*pehrmeetahmeh prehsehntahrleh ah...*
This is my wife/daughter/mother/girlfriend	Esta es mi esposa/mi hija/mi mamá/mi amiga	*ehstah ehs mee ehspohsah/mee eehah /mee mahmah/mee ahmeegah*
– my husband/son/father/boyfriend	Este es mi marido/mi hijo/mi papá/mi amigo	*ehsteh ehs mee mahreedoh/mee eehoh/mee pahpah/mee ahmeegoh*
How do you do	Hola, mucho gusto	*ohlah, moochoh goostoh*
Pleased to meet you	Encantado(a) (de conocerlo/a)	*ehnkahntahdoh(ah) (deh kohnohsehrloh/ah)*
Where are you from?	¿De dónde es usted?	*deh dohndeh ehs oostehdh?*
I'm from England/Scotland/Ireland/Wales	Soy inglés/esa escocés/esa irlandés/esa galés/esa	*soy eenglehs/ehsah ehskohsehs/ehsah eerlahndehs/ehsah gahlehs/ ehsah*
What city do you live in?	¿En qué ciudad vive?	*ehn keh syoodahdh beebeh?*
In..., It's near...	En...Eso está cerca de...	*ehn...ehstah sehrkah deh...*
Have you been here long?	¿Hace mucho que está aquí?	*ahseh moochoh keh ehstah ahkee?*
A few days	Unos días	*oonohs deeahs*
How long are you staying here?	¿Cuánto tiempo piensa quedarse?	*kwahntoh tyehmpoh pyehnsah kehdahrseh?*
We're (probably) leaving tomorrow/in two weeks	Nos iremos (probablemente) mañana/dentro de dos semanas	*nohs eerehmohs (prohbahblehmehnteh) mahnyahnah/dehntroh deh dohs sehmahnahs*
Where are you staying?	¿Dónde se aloja?	*dohndeh seh ahlohhah?*
In a hotel/an apartment	En un hotel/departamento	*ehn oon ohtehl/dehpahrtahmehntoh*
On a camp site	En un camping	*ehn oon kahmpeen*
With friends/relatives	En casa de amigos/parientes	*ehn kahsah deh ahmeegohs/pahryehntehs*
Are you here on your own/with your family?	¿Vino solo(a)/con su familia?	*beenoh sohloh(ah)/kohn soo fahmeelyah?*

I'm on my own — Vine solo(a)
beeneh sohloh(ah)

I'm with my partner/wife/husband — con mi pareja/esposa/marido
kohn mee pahrehhah/ehspohsah/mahreedoh

– with my family — con mi familia
kohn mee fahmeelyah

– with relatives — con unos parientes
kohn oonohs pahryehntehs

– with a friend/friends — con un amigo/una amiga/unos amigos
kohn oon ahmeegoh/oonah ahmeegah/oonohs ahmeegohs

Are you married? — ¿Está casado/casada?
ehstah kahsahdoh/kahsahdah?

Do you have a steady boyfriend/girlfriend? — ¿Tienes novio/novia?
tyehnehs nohbyoh/nohbyah?

That's none of your business — ¿Qué le importa?
keh leh eempohrtah?

I'm married — Soy casado
soy kahsahdoh

– single — Soy soltero
soy sohltehroh

– separated — Estoy separado
ehstoy sehpahrahdoh

– divorced — Estoy divorciado
ehstoy deebohrsyahdoh

– a widow/widower — Soy viuda/viudo
soy byoodah/byoodoh

I live alone/with someone — Vivo solo(a)/con otra persona
beeboh sohloh(ah)/kohn ohtrah pehrsohnah

Do you have any children/grandchildren? — ¿Tiene hijos/nietos?
tyehneh eehohs/nyehtohs?

How old are you? — ¿Cuántos años tiene?
kwahntohs ahnyohs tyehneh?

How old is she/he? — ¿Cuántos años tiene?
kwahntohs ahnyohs tyehneh?

I'm... — Tengo...años
tehngoh...ahnyohs

She's/he's... — Tiene...años
tyehneh...ahnyohs

What do you do for a living? — ¿En qué trabaja?
ehn keh trahbahhah?

I work in an office — Trabajo en una oficina
trahbahhoh ehn oonah ohfeeseenah

I'm a student/ I'm at school — Estudio
ehstoodyoh

I'm unemployed — No tengo trabajo
noh tehngoh trahbahhoh

I'm retired — Soy jubilado
soy hoobeelahdoh

I'm on a disability pension — Tengo una pensión de invalidez
tehngoh oonah pehnsyohn deh eenbahleedes

I'm a housewife — Soy ama de casa
soy ahmah deh kahsah

Do you like your job?	¿Le gusta su trabajo? *leh goostah soo trahbahhoh?*
Most of the time	Casi siempre *kahsee syehmpreh*
I usually do, but I prefer holidays	Por lo general sí, pero prefiero las vacaciones *pohr loh hehnehrahl see, pehroh prehfyehroh lahs bahkahsyohnehs*

3.3 Starting/ending a conversation

Could I ask you something?	¿Podría preguntarle una cosa? *pohdreeah prehgoontahrleh oonah kohsah?*
Excuse me	Perdone *pehrdohneh*
Excuse me, could you help me?	¿Podría ayudarme? *pohdreeah ahyoodahrmeh?*
Yes, what's the problem?	Sí, ¿qué pasa? *see, keh pahsah?*
What can I do for you?	¿En qué puedo servirlo/a? *ehn keh pwehdoh sehrbeerloh/ah?*
Sorry, I don't have time now	Lo siento, ahora no tengo tiempo *loh syehntoh, ahohrah noh tehngoh tyehmpoh*
Do you have a light?	¿Tiene fuego? *tyehneh fwehgoh?*
May I join you?	¿Me puedo sentar? *meh pwehdoh sehntahr?*
Could you take a picture of me/us? Press this button	¿Podría sacarme/sacarnos una foto? Hay que apretar este botón *pohdreeah sahkahrmeh/sahkahrnohs oonah fohtoh? ay keh ahprehtahr ehsteh bohtohn*
Leave me alone	Déjeme en paz *dehhehmeh ehn pahs*
Get lost	Váyase al diablo *bahyahseh ahl deeahbloh*
Go away or I'll scream	Como no se vaya, grito *kohmoh noh seh bahyah, greetoh*

3.4 Congratulations and condolences

Happy birthday/many happy returns	Feliz cumpleaños/felicidades *fehlees koomplehahnyohs/fehleeseedahdehs*
Please accept my condolences	Lo/a acompaño en el sentimiento *loh/ah ahkohmpahnyoh ehn ehl sehnteemyehntoh*
I'm very sorry for you	¡Cuánto lo siento por usted! *kwahntoh loh syehntoh pohr oostehdh!*

3.5 A chat about the weather

See also 1.5 The weather

It's so hot/cold today!	¡Qué calor/frío hace hoy! *keh kahlohr/freeoh ahseh oy!*
Nice weather, isn't it?	¡Qué buen tiempo hace! ¿Verdad? *keh bwehn tyehmpoh ahseh! behrdadh?*

What a wind/storm!	¡Vaya viento/tormenta! *bahyah byehntoh/tohrmentah!*
All that rain/snow!	¡Cómo llueve/nieva! *kohmoh lywehbeh/nyehbah!*
All that fog!	¡Cuánta niebla! *kwahntah nyehblah!*
Has the weather been like this for long here?	¿Hace mucho que hace este tiempo? *ahseh moochoh keh ahseh ehsteh tyehmpoh?*
Is it always this hot/cold here?	¿Aquí siempre hace tanto calor/frío? *ahkee syehmpreh ahseh tahntoh kahlohr/freeoh?*
Is it always this dry/wet here?	¿Aquí siempre hace un tiempo tan seco/lluvioso? *ahkee syehmpreh ahseh oon tyehmpoh tahn sehkoh/lyoobyohsoh?*

3.6 Hobbies

Do you have any hobbies?	¿Tiene algún hobby? *tyehneh ahlgoon hohbee?*
I like painting/reading/photography/DIY	Me gusta pintar/leer/la fotografía/el bricolaje *meh goostah peentahr/lehehr/lah fohtohgrahfeeah/ehl breekohlahheh*
I like music	Me gusta la música *meh goostah lah mooseekah*
I like playing the guitar/piano	Me gusta tocar la guitarra/el piano *meh goostah tohkahr lah gueetahrrah/ehl pyahnoh*
I like going to the movies	Me gusta ir al cine *meh goostah eer ahl seeneh*
I like travelling/sport/fishing/walking	Me gusta viajar/hacer deporte/pescar/salir a caminar *meh goostah byahhahr/ahsehr dehpohrteh/pehskahr/sahleer ah kahmeenahr*

3.7 Being the host(ess)

See also 4 Eating out

Can I offer you a drink?	¿Le gustaría algo de beber? *leh goostahreeah ahlgoh deh behbehr?*
What would you like to drink?	¿Qué quieres beber? *keh kyehrehs behbehr?*
Something non-alcoholic, please	Algo sin alcohol *ahlgoh seen ahlkohl*
Would you like a cigarette/cigar/to roll your own?	¿Quiere un cigarro/un puro/liar un cigarrillo? *kyehreh oon seegahrroh/oon pooroh/leeahr oon seegahrroh?*
I don't smoke	No fumo *noh foomoh*

3.8 Invitations

Are you doing anything tonight?	*¿Tiene algo que hacer esta noche?* *tyehneh ahlgoh keh ahsehr ehstah nohcheh?*
Do you have any plans for today/this afternoon/tonight?	*¿Ya tiene planes para hoy/esta tarde/esta noche?* *yah tyehneh plahnehs pahrah oy/ehstah tahrdeh/ehstah nohcheh?*
Would you like to go out with me?	*¿Quieres salir conmigo?* *kyehrehs sahleer kohnmeegoh?*
Would you like to go dancing with me?	*¿Quieres ir a bailar conmigo?* *kyehrehs eer ah baylahr kohnmeegoh?*
Would you like to have lunch/dinner with me?	*¿Quieres ir a comer/cenar conmigo?* *kyehrehs eer ah kohmehr/sehnahr kohnmeegoh?*
Would you like to come to the beach with me?	*¿Quieres ir a la playa conmigo?* *kyehrehs eer ah lah plahyah kohnmeegoh?*
Would you like to come into town with us?	*¿Quieres ir a la ciudad con nosotros?* *kyehrehs eer ah lah thyoodahdh kohn nohsohtrohs?*
Would you like to come and see some friends with us?	*¿Quieres ir a casa de unos amigos con nosotros?* *kyehrehs eer ah kahsah deh oonohs ahmeegohs kohn nohsohtrohs?*
Shall we dance?	*¿Bailamos?* *baylahmohs?*
– sit at the bar?	*¿Vienes a sentarte conmigo en la barra?* *byehnehs ah sehntahrteh kohnmeegoh ehn lah bahrrah?*
– get something to drink?	*¿Vamos a beber algo?* *bahmohs ah behbehr ahlgoh?*
– go for a walk/drive?	*¿Vamos a dar una vuelta?* *bahmohs ah dahr oonah bwehltah?*
Yes, all right	*Sí, vamos* *see, bahmohs*
Good idea	*Buena idea* *bwehnah eedehah*
No (thank you)	*No (gracias)* *noh (grahsyahs)*
Maybe later	*Quizá más tarde* *keesah mahs tahrdeh*
I don't feel like it	*No tengo ganas* *noh tehngoh gahnahs*
I don't have time	*No tengo tiempo* *noh tehngoh tyehmpoh*
I already have a date	*Ya tengo otro compromiso* *yah tehngoh ohtroh kohmprohmeesoh*
I'm not very good at dancing/volleyball/swimming	*No sé bailar/jugar al vóleibol/nadar* *noh seh baylahr/hoogahr ahl vohleheebohl/nahdahr*

3.9 Paying a compliment

You look wonderful!	*¡Te ves muy bien!* *teh behs mwee byehn!*
I like your car!	*¡Qué bonito coche!* *keh bohneetoh kohcheh!*

I like your ski outfit!	¡Qué bonito traje de esquiar!	*keh bohneetoh trahheh deh ehskeeahr!*
You're a nice boy/girl	Eres muy bueno/buena	*ehrehs mwee bwehnoh/bwehnah*
What a sweet child!	¡Qué niño tan lindo/niña tan linda!	*keh neenyoh tahn leendoh/neenyah tahn leendah!*
You're a wonderful dancer!	Bailas muy bien	*bahylahs mwee byehn*
You're a wonderful cook!	Cocinas muy bien	*kohseenahs mwee byehn*
You're a terrific soccer player!	Juegas muy bien al fútbol	*hwehgahs mwee byehn ahl footbohl*

Conversation

3.10 Chatting someone up

I like being with you	Me gusta estar contigo	*meh goostah ehstahr kohnteegoh*
I've missed you so much	Te extrañé mucho	*teh ehkstrahnyeh moochoh*
I dreamt about you	Soñé contigo	*sohnyeh kohnteegoh*
I think about you all day	Pienso todo el día en ti	*pyehnsoh tohdoh ehl deeah ehn tee*
You have such a sweet smile	Tienes una sonrisa muy bonita	*tyehnehs oonah sohnreesah mwee bohneetah*
You have such beautiful eyes	Tienes unos ojos muy bonitos	*tyehnehs oonohs ohhohs mwee bohneetohs*
I'm in love with you	Estoy enamorado/enamorada de ti	*ehstoy ehnahmohrahdoh/ehnahmohrahdah deh tee*
I'm in love with you too	Yo también de ti	*yoh tahmbyehn deh tee*
I love you	Te quiero	*teh kyehroh*
I love you too	Yo también a ti	*yoh tahmbyehn ah tee*
I don't feel as strongly about you	Yo no siento lo mismo por ti	*yoh noh syehntoh loh meesmoh pohr tee*
I already have a boyfriend/girlfriend	Ya tengo novio/a	*yah tehngoh nohbyoh/ah*
I'm not ready for that	Yo no estoy preparado(a)	*yoh noh ehstoy prehpahrahdoh/ah*
This is going too fast for me	Vamos demasiado rápido	*bahmohs dehmahsyahdoh rahpeedoh*
Take your hands off me	No me toque(s)	*noh meh tohkeh(s)*
Okay, no problem	No importa	*noh eempohrtah*
Will you stay with me tonight?	¿Te quedas a dormir?	*teh kehdahs ah dohrmeer?*
I'd like to go to bed with you	Me gustaría acostarme contigo	*meh goostahreeah ahkohstahrmeh kohnteegoh*

Only if we use a condom — Sólo si usamos condón
sohloh see oosahmohs kohndohn

We have to be careful about AIDS — Hay que tener cuidado por lo del Sida
ay keh tehnehr kweedahdoh pohr loh dehl seedah

That's what they all say — Eso es lo que dicen todos
ehsoh ehs loh keh deesehn tohdohs

We shouldn't take any risks — Más vale no arriesgarse
mahs bahleh noh ahrryehsgahrseh

Do you have a condom? — ¿Tienes condones?
tyehnehs kohndohnehs?

No? In that case we won't do it — ¿No? Pues entonces no
noh? pwehs ehntohnsehs noh

3.11 Arrangements

When will I see you again? — ¿Cuándo nos volvemos a ver?
kwahndoh nohs bohlbehmohs ah behr?

Are you free over the weekend? — ¿Tiene tiempo este fin de semana?
tyehneh tyehmpoh ehsteh feen deh sehmahnah?

What shall we arrange? — ¿Cómo quedamos?
kohmoh kehdahmohs?

Where shall we meet? — ¿Dónde nos encontramos?
dohndeh nohs ehnkohntrahmohs?

Will you pick me/us up? — ¿Me/nos pasa a buscar?
meh/nohs pahsah ah booskahr?

Shall I pick you up? — ¿Lo/la paso a buscar?
loh/lah pahsoh ah booskahr?

I have to be home by... — Tengo que estar en casa a las...
tehngoh keh ehstahr ehn kahsah ah lahs...

I don't want to see you anymore — No quiero volver a verlo/verla
noh kyehroh bohlbehr ah behrloh/behrlah

3.12 Saying goodbye

Can I take you home? — ¿Lo/la acompaño a su casa?
loh/lah ahkohmpahnyoh ah soo kahsah?

Can I write/call you? — ¿Puedo escribirle/llamarlo/llamarla por teléfono?
pwehdoh ehskreebeerleh /lyahmahrloh/ lyahmahrlah pohr tehlehfohnoh?

Will you write/call me? — ¿Me escribirá/llamará por teléfono?
meh ehskreebeerah/lyahmahrah pohr tehlehfohnoh?

Can I have your address/phone number? — ¿Me da su dirección/número de teléfono?
meh dah soo deerehksyohn/noomehroh deh tehlehfohnoh?

Thanks for everything — Gracias por todo
grahsyahs pohr tohdoh

It was very nice — Lo hemos pasado muy bien
loh ehmohs pahsahdoh mwee byehn

Say hello to... — Saludos a...
sahloodohs ah...

All the best — Te deseo lo mejor
teh dehsehoh loh mehhohr

Good luck	Buena suerte *bwehnah swehrteh*
When will you be back?	¿Cuándo regresas? *kwahndoh rehgrehsahs?*
I'll be waiting for you	Te esperaré *teh ehspehrahreh*
I'd like to see you again	Me gustaría volver a verte *meh goostahreeah bohlbehr ah behrteh*
I hope we meet again soon	Espero que nos volvamos a ver pronto *ehspehroh keh nohs bohlbahmohs ah behr prohntoh*
This is our address. If you're ever in the UK	Esta es nuestra dirección. Si alguna vez pasa por el Reino Unido... *ehstah ehs nwehstrah deerehksyohn. see ahlgoonah behs pahsah pohr ehl reheenoh ooneedoh...*
You'd be more than welcome	Está cordialmente invitado *ehstah kohrdyahlmehnteh eenbeetahdoh*

4

Eating out

4 Eating out

● **In Latin American countries** people usually have three meals:
1 *El desayuno* (breakfast) approximately between 7 and 9am. Breakfast is light and consists of *café con leche* (white coffee), croissants or *tostadas* (toast).
2 *El almuerzo* (lunch) approx. between 12 and 2pm. Lunch always includes a hot dish and is the most important meal of the day. Office workers and schoolchildren still lunch at home. It usually consists of four courses:
– starter (which can be a plate of greens)
– main course
– dessert
– fruit
3 *La cena* (dinner) between 8 and 10pm. Dinner is usually a light, hot meal, taken with the family.
At around 5pm, a snack (*la merienda, called 'once' in Chile*) is often served.

4.1 On arrival

I'd like to book a table for seven o'clock, please	¿Podría reservar una mesa para las siete? *pohdreeah rehsehrbahr oonah mehsah pahrah lahs syehteh?*
I'd like a table for two, please	Quisiera una mesa para dos personas *keesyehrah oonah mehsah pahrah dohs pehrsohnahs*
We've/we haven't booked	(No) hemos reservado *(noh) ehmohs rehsehrbahdoh*
Is the restaurant open yet?	¿Ya está abierto el restaurante? *yah ehstah ahbyehrtoh ehl rehstahoorahnteh?*
What time does the restaurant open/close?	¿A qué hora abre/cierra el restaurante? *ah keh ohrah ahbreh/syehrah ehl rehstahoorahnteh?*
Can we wait for a table?	¿Podemos esperar hasta que se desocupe una mesa? *pohdehmohs ehspehrahr ahstah keh seh dehsohkoopeh oonah mehsah?*
Do we have to wait long?	¿Tenemos que esperar mucho? *tehnehmohs keh ehspehrahr moochoh?*
Is this seat taken?	¿Está ocupada esta silla? *ehstah ohkoopahdah ehstah seelyah?*
Could we sit here/there?	¿Podemos sentarnos aquí/allí? *pohdemohs sehntahrnohs ahkee/ahlyee?*

¿Ha reservado mesa?	Do you have a reservation?
¿A nombre de quién?	What name, please?
Por aquí, por favor.	This way, please
Esta mesa está reservada	This table is reserved
En quince minutos quedará libre una mesa	We'll have a table free in fifteen minutes.
¿Le importaría esperar (en la barra)	Would you like to wait (at the bar)?

Can we sit by the window?	¿Podemos sentarnos junto a la ventana? *pohdehmohs sehntahrnohs hoontoh ah lah behntahnah?*
Can we eat outside?	¿Podemos comer afuera? *pohdehmohs kohmehr ahfwehrah?*
Do you have another chair for us?	¿Podría traernos otra silla? *pohdreeah trahehrnohs ohtrah seelyah?*
Do you have a highchair?	¿Podría traernos una silla para niños? *pohdreeah trahehrnohs oonah seelyah pahrah neenyohs?*
Is there a socket for this bottle-warmer?	¿Hay un enchufe para este calentador de biberones? *ay oon ehnchoofeh pahrah ehsteh kahlehntahdohr deh beebehrohnehs?*
Could you warm up this bottle/jar for me?	¿Podría calentarme este biberón/este bote? *pohdreeah kahlehntahrmeh ehsteh beebehrohn/ehsteh bohteh?*
Not too hot, please	Que no esté muy caliente, por favor *keh noh ehsteh mwee kahlyehnteh pohr fahbohr*
Is there somewhere I can change the baby's nappy?	¿Hay algún lugar para cambiar al bebé? *ay ahlgoon loogahr pahrah kahmbyahr ahl behbeh?*
Where are the toilets?	¿Dónde están los baños/aseos? *dohnde ehstahn lohs bahnyos/ahsehohs?*

4.2 Ordering

Waiter!	¡Mozo (mesero)! *mohsoh (mehsehroh)!*
Madam!/Sir!	¡Oiga, (por favor)! *oygah (pohr fahbohr)!*
We'd like something to eat/a drink	Quisiéramos comer/beber algo *keesyehrahmohs kohmehr/behber ahlgoh*
Could I have a quick meal?	¿Podría comer algo rápido? *pohdreeah kohmehr ahlgoh rahpeedoh?*
We don't have much time	Tenemos poco tiempo *tehnehmohs pohkoh tyehmpoh*
We'd like to have a drink first	Antes quisiéramos beber algo *ahntehs keesyehrahmohs behbehr ahlgoh*
Could we see the menu/wine list, please?	¿Nos podría traer la carta/la carta de vinos? *nohs pohdreeah trahehr lah kahrtah/lah kahrtah deh beenohs?*
Do you have a menu in English?	¿Tienen menú en inglés? *tyehnehn mehnoo ehn eenglehs?*
Do you have a dish of the day?	¿Tienen menú del día/menú turístico? *tyehnehn mehnoo dehl deeah/mehnoo tooreesteekoh?*
We haven't made a choice yet	Todavía no hemos elegido *tohdahbeeah noh ehmohs ehlehheedoh*
What do you recommend?	¿Qué nos recomienda? *keh nohs rehkohmyehndah?*

What are the specialities of the region/the house?	¿Cuáles son las especialidades de la región/de la casa? *kwahlehs sohn lahs ehspehsyahleedahdehs deh lah rehhyohn/deh lah kahsah?*
I like strawberries/olives	Me gustan las fresas/las aceitunas *meh goostahn lahs frehsahs/lahs ahseheetoonahs*
I don't like meat/fish/...	No me gusta el pescado/la carne/... *noh meh goostah ehl pehskahdoh/lah kahrneh/...*
What's this?	¿Qué es esto? *keh ehs ehstoh?*
Does it have...in it?	¿Tiene...? *tyehneh...?*
What does it taste like?	¿A qué sabe? *ah keh sahbeh?*
Is this a hot or a cold dish?	¿Es un plato caliente o frío? *ehs oon plahtoh kahlyehnyteh oh freeoh?*
Is this sweet?	¿Es un plato dulce? *ehs oon plahtoh doolse?*
Is this spicy?	¿Es un plato picante? *ehs oon plahtoh peekahnteh?*
Do you have anything else, please?	¿Tendría otra cosa? *tehndreeah ohtrah kohsah?*
I'm on a salt-free diet	No puedo comer sal *noh pwehdoh kohmehr sahl*
I can't eat pork	No puedo comer carne de cerdo *noh pwehdoh kohmehr kahrneh deh sehrdoh*
– sugar	No puedo comer azúcar *noh pwehdo kohmehr ahsookahr*
– fatty foods	No puedo comer grasa *noh pwehdoh kohmehr grahsah*
– (hot) spices	No puedo comer cosas picantes *noh pwehdoh kohmehr kohsahs peekahntehs*
I'll/we'll have what those people are having	Lo mismo que esos señores, por favor *loh meesmoh keh ehsohs sehnyohrehs pohr fahbohr*
I'd like...	Para mí... *pahrah mee...*

¿Van a tomar un aperitivo?	Would you like a drink first?
¿Ya han elegido?	Have you decided?
¿Qué van a tomar?	What would you like to eat?
Que aproveche	Enjoy your meal.
¿Quiere su bistec rojo, mediano o bien?	Would you like your steak rare, medium or well done?
¿Van a comer postre/tomar café?	Would you like a dessert/coffee?

We're not having a starter	No vamos a comer entrada *noh bahmohs ah kohmehr ehntrahdah*
The child will share what we're having	El niño/la niña comerá de nuestro menú *ehl neenyoh/lah neenyah kohmehrah deh nwehstroh mehnoo*
Could I have some more bread, please?	Más pan, por favor *mahs pahn pohr fahbohr*
– a bottle of water/wine	Otra botella de agua/de vino, por favor *ohtrah bohtehlyah deh ahgwah/deh beenoh, pohr fahbohr*
– another helping of...	Otra ración de..., por favor *ohtrah rahsyohn deh..., pohr fahbohr*
– some salt and pepper	¿Podría traerme sal y pimienta? *pohdreeah trahehrmeh sahl ee peemyehntah?*
– a napkin	¿Podría traerme una servilleta? *pohdreeah trahehrmeh oonah sehrbeelyehtah?*
– a spoon	¿Podría traerme una cuchara? *pohdreeah trahehrmeh oonah koochahrah?*
– an ashtray	¿Podría traerme un cenicero? *pohdreeah trahehrmeh oon sehneesehroh?*
– some matches	¿Podría traerme cerillas fósforos? *pohdreeah trahehrmeh sehreelyahs fohsfohrohs?*
– some toothpicks	¿Podría traerme unos palillos? *pohdreeah trahehrmeh oonohs pahleelyohs?*
– a glass of water	¿Podría traerme un vaso de agua? *pohdreeah trahehrmeh oon bahsoh deh ahgwah?*
– a straw (for the child)	¿Podría traerme una pajita (para el niño/la niña)? *pohdreeah trahehrmeh oonah pahheetah (pahrah ehl neenyoh/lah neenyah)?*
Enjoy your meal!	¡Que aproveche! *keh ahprohbehcheh!*
You too!	Igualmente *eegwahlmehnteh*
Cheers!	¡Salud! *sahloodh!*
The next round's on me	La próxima ronda me toca a mí *lah prohxeemah rohndah meh tohkah ah mee*
Could we have a doggy bag, please?	¿Podemos llevarnos las sobras? *pohdehmohs lyehbarnohs lahs sohbrahs?*

4.3 The bill

See also 8.2 Settling the bill

How much is this dish?	¿Cuánto vale este plato? *kwahntoh bahleh ehsteh plahtoh?*
Could I have the bill, please?	La cuenta, por favor *lah kwehntah, pohr fahbohr*
All together	Todo junto *tohdoh hoontoh*
Everyone pays separately	Cada uno paga lo suyo *kahdah oonoh pahgah loh sooyoh*

Could we have the menu again, please?	¿Podría traernos otra vez la carta? *pohdreeah trahehrnohs ohtrah behs lah kahrtah?*
The...is not on the bill	Olvidó apuntar el/la... *olbeedoh ahpoontahr ehl/lah...*

4.4 Complaints

It's taking a very long time	Están tardando mucho *ehstahn tahrdahndoh moochoh*
We've been here an hour already	Ya llevamos una hora aquí *yah lyebahmohs oonah ohrah ahkee*
This must be a mistake	Esto tiene que ser una equivocación *ehstoh tyehneh keh sehr oonah ehkeebohkahsyohn*
This is not what I ordered	Esto no es lo que pedí *ehstoh noh ehs loh keh pehdee*
I ordered...	Pedí... *pehdee*
There's a dish missing	Falta un plato *fahltah oon plahtoh*
This is broken/not clean	Esto está roto/no está limpio *ehstoh ehstah rohtoh/noh ehstah leempyoh*
The food's cold	La comida está fría *lah kohmeedah ehstah freeah*
– not fresh	La comida no es fresca *lah kohmeedah noh ehs frehskah*
– too salty/sweet/spicy	La comida está muy salada/dulce/picante *lah kohmeedah ehstah mwee sahlahdah/doolseh/peekahnteh*
The meat's not done	La carne está cruda *lah kahrneh ehstah kroodah*
– overdone	La carne está muy cocida *lah kahrneh ehstah mwee kohseedah*
– tough	La carne está dura *lah kahrneh ehstah doorah*
– off	La carne está podrida *lah kahrneh ehstah pohdreedah*
Could I have something else instead of this?	¿Me podría traer otra cosa en lugar de esto? *meh pohdreeah trahehr ohtrah kohsah ehn loogahr deh ehstoh?*
The bill/this amount is not right	La cuenta/este precio está mal *lah kwehntah/ehsteh prehsyoh ehstah mahl*
We didn't have this	Esto no lo hemos comido/bebido *ehstoh noh loh ehmohs kohmeedoh/behbeedoh*
There's no paper in the toilet	No hay papel en el baño *noh ay pahpehl ehn ehl bahnyoh*
Do you have a complaints book?	¿Tienen libro de quejas? *tyehnen leebroh deh kehhas?*
Will you call the manager, please?	Haga el favor de llamar al jefe *ahgah ehl fahbohr deh lyamahr ahl hehfeh*

4.5 Paying a compliment

That was a wonderful meal — **Comimos muy bien**
kohmeemohs mwee byehn

The food was excellent — **La comida ha estado exquisita**
lah kohmeedah ah ehstahdoh ehxkeeseetah

The...in particular was delicious — **Sobre todo nos gustó el/la...**
sohbreh tohdoh nohs goostoh ehl/lah...

4.6 The menu

aperitivo
apéritif
aves
poultry
azúcar
sugar
bebidas alcohólicas
alcoholic beverages
bebidas calientes
hot beverages
carta de vinos
wine list
cócteles
cocktails
cubierto
cover charge
entremeses variados
hors d'oeuvres
mariscos
seafood
pastelería
pastry
pescados
fish
platos calientes
hot dishes
platos combinados
combined dishes
plato del día
dish of the day
platos fríos
cold dishes
platos principales
main courses
platos típicos
regional specialities
postres
sweets/dessert
primeros platos
starters
raciones
portions
servicio incluido
service included
sopas
soups
tapas
tapas
venado
game
verduras
vegetables

4.7 Alphabetical list of drinks and dishes

aceituna
olive
aguacate/palta
avocado
ajo
garlic
albóndigas
meat balls
alcachofa/alcaucil
artichoke
almejas
clams
almendras
almonds
ancas de rana
frog's legs
anchoa/boquerón
anchovy
anguila
eel
anís
aniseed
apio
celery
arenque
herring
arroz
rice
asado
roast, roasted
atún/bonito
tuna
avellana
hazelnut
bacalao
cod
barbacoa asado
barbecued meat
licuado/batido de...
...milk shake
berenjena
aubergine
biftec/bife/bistec
steak
bizcocho
sponge cake
blanquillo/huevo
egg
buey/vaca
beef
cabrito
kid
café (solo/con leche)
coffee (black/white)
calamares (en su tinta)
squid (cooked in their ink)
caldo
broth

callos
tripe
cangrejo
crab
caracoles
snails
carne
meat
carpa
carp
castaña
chestnut
cebolla
onion
cerdo/puerco
pork
cerezas
cherries
cerveza
beer
ceviche
marinated raw seafood
chile
chilli pepper
chorizo
chorizo (paprika flavoured salami sausage)
chucrut
sauerkraut
chuleta/costilla
chop
churros
fritters
ciervo
venison
cigalas
Dublin Bay prawns
ciruela
plum
cochinillo asado
roast suckling pig
cocido
boiled
codorniz
quail
col/berza/repollo
cabbage
coles repollitos de Bruselas
Brussels sprouts
coliflor
cauliflower
coñac
brandy
conejo
rabbit
copa helada/helado
ice cream
cordero
lamb
crema/nata
cream
criadillas/mollejas
sweetbreads
crudo
raw
cuba libre
rum coke
dátil
date
dulce
sweet
enchiladas
stuffed tortillas
en escabeche
pickled
endibia
chicory/endive
ensalada (mixta)
mixed salad
ensaladilla rusa
Russian salad
escalope
escalope
espárragos
asparagus
especias
spices
espinaca
spinach
fideos
noodles
filete
fillet
flan
cream caramel
frambuesa
raspberry
fresa/frutilla
strawberry
frito
fried
fruta (del tiempo)
seasonal fruit
galleta
biscuit
gambas/camarones
prawns
garbanzos
chick peas
gazpacho andaluz
gazpacho (cold soup)
granizado de limón/café
iced drink (lemon/coffee)
grosellas
red/black currants
guacamole
avocado dip
guisado
stew
guisantes/arvejas
peas
habas
broad beans
harina
flour
hígado de ganso
goose liver
higo
fig
huevos al plato/ duros/revueltos
fried/hard boiled/scrambled eggs
jamón de York/serrano
ham (cooked/Parma style)
jerez (seco, dulce)
sherry (dry, sweet)
jugo
fruit juice
langosta
lobster
langostino
crayfish
leche
milk
lechuga
lettuce
legumbres
vegetables (legumes)
lengua
tongue

lenguado
sole

lentejas
lentils

licor
liqueur

liebre
hare

limón
lemon

lomo de cerdo/puerco
tenderloin of pork

maíz (mazorca)/elote/choclo
corn (on the cob)

mantequilla
butter

manzana
apple

mazapán
marzipan

mejillones
mussels

melocotón durazno (en almíbar)
peach (in syrup)

melón
melon

membrillo
quince

merluza
hake

mermelada
jam

mero
sea bass

mole
chilli and chocolate sauce

morcilla
black pudding

mostaza
mustard

muslo de pollo
drumstick

nuez
walnut

ostras
oysters

paella
paella

pan
bread

pastel/queque
cake

papas/patatas fritas
chips/crisps

pato (silvestre)
(wild) duck

pechuga (de pollo)
(chicken) breast

pepino
cucumber

pepinillos
gherkins

pera
pear

perdiz
partridge

perejil
parsley

pescado
fish

picadillo de ternera
minced veal

pierna (de cordero)
leg (of lamb)

pimentón/chile
paprika

pimienta
pepper

pimientos
green/red peppers

piña
pineapple

plancha (a la)
grilled

plátano/banana
banana

plato principal
main course

platos típicos
regional specialities

pollo
chicken

puerro/poro
leek

pulpo
octopus

queso
cheese

rábanos
radishes

rabo de buey
oxtail

rape
monkfish

remolacha
beetroot

riñones
kidneys

rodaballo
turbot

romana (a la)
deep fried

vino rosado
rosé wine

salchicha
sausage

salchichón/salame
salami

salmón
salmon

salmón ahumado
smoked salmon

salmonete
red mullet

sandía
water melon

sandwich
sandwich

sangría
sangría

sardinas
sardines

setas/champiñones
mushrooms

solomillo/lomo de buey/vaca
fillet of beef

sopa
soup

taco
stuffed maize/corn pancake

tarta helada
ice cream cake

tequila
tequila

ternera
veal

tinto
red wine

tocino
bacon

tortilla
maize/corn pancake

tortilla española
Spanish omelette (potato)

tortilla francesa
plain omelette
tortitas
waffles
trucha
trout
trufas
truffles

turrón
nougat
uvas
grapes
vainitas/chauchas
French beans
verduras
green vegetables

vinagre
vinegar
zanahorias
carrots
jugo de naranja
orange juice

5

On the road

5 On the road

5.1 Asking for directions

Excuse me, could I ask you something?	Perdone, ¿podría preguntarle algo? *pehrdohneh, pohdreeah prehgoontahrleh ahlgoh?*
I've lost my way	Me he perdido *meh eh pehrdeedoh*
Is there a(n)... around here?	¿Sabe dónde hay un(a)...por aquí? *sahbeh dohndeh ay oon(ah)...pohr ahkee?*
Is this the way to...?	¿Se va por aquí a...? *seh bah pohr ahkee ah...?*
Could you tell me how to get to the... (name of place) by car/on foot?	¿Podría decirme cómo llegar a... (en coche/a pie)? *pohdreeah dehseermeh kohmoh lyehgahr ah... (ehn kohcheh/ah pyeh)?*
What's the quickest way to...?	¿Cómo hago para llegar lo antes posible a...? *kohmoh ahgoh pahrah lyehgahr loh ahntehs pohseebleh ah...?*
How many kilometres is it to...?	¿Cuántos kilómetros faltan para llegar a...? *kwahntohs keelohmehtrohs fahltahn pahrah lyehgahr ah...?*
Could you point it out on the map?	¿Podría señalarlo en el mapa? *pohdreeah sehnyahlahrloh ehn ehl mahpah?*

No sé; no soy de aquí	I don't know, I don't know my way around here
Por aquí no es	You're going the wrong way
Tiene que volver a...	You have to go back to...
Allí los carteles le indicarán	From there on just follow the signs
Vuelva a preguntar allí	When you get there, ask again

derecho straight ahead	la calle the street	el viaducto the fly-over
a la izquierda left	el semáforo the traffic light	el puente the bridge
a la derecha right	el túnel the tunnel	el paso a nivel/ las barreras the level crossing/ the boom gates
doblar turn	el stop the 'give way' sign	el cartel en dirección de... the sign pointing to...
seguir follow	el edificio the building	la flecha the arrow
cruzar cross	en la esquina at the corner	
el cruce the intersection	el río the river	

Su pasaporte, por favor	Your passport, please
La tarjeta verde, por favor	Your green card, please
El permiso de circulación/la carta gris, por favor	Your vehicle documents, please
¿Adónde va?	Where are you heading?
¿Cuánto tiempo piensa quedarse?	How long are you planning to stay?
¿Tiene algo que declarar?	Do you have anything to declare?
¿Puede abrir esto?	Open this, please

My children are entered on this passport	Mis hijos están registrados en este pasaporte *mees eehohs ehstahn rehheestrahdohs ehn ehsteh pahsahpohrteh*
I'm travelling through	Estoy de paso *ehstoy deh pahsoh*
I'm going on holiday to...	Voy de vacaciones a... *boy deh bahkahsyohnehs ah...*
I'm on a business trip	He venido en viaje de negocios *eh behneedoh ehn byahheh deh nehgohsyohs*
I don't know how long I'll be staying yet	Todavía no sé cuánto tiempo me quedaré *tohdahbeeah noh seh kwahntoh tyehmpoh meh kehdahreh*
I'll be staying here for a weekend	Pienso quedarme un fin de semana *pyehnsoh kehdahrmeh oon feen deh sehmahnah*
– for a few days	Pienso quedarme unos días *pyehnsoh kehdahrmeh oonohs deeahs*
– for a week	Pienso quedarme una semana *pyehnsoh kehdahrmeh oonah sehmahnah*
– for two weeks	Pienso quedarme dos semanas *pyehnsoh kehdahrmeh dohs sehmahnahs*
I've got nothing to declare	No tengo nada que declarar *noh tehngoh nahdah keh dehklahrahr*
I've got...with me	Traigo... *trahygoh...*
– ...cartons of cigarettes	Traigo...cartones de cigarros *trahygoh...kahrtohnehs deh seegahrrohs*
– ...bottles of...	Traigo...botellas de... *trahygoh...bohtehlyahs deh...*
– some souvenirs	Traigo algunos recuerdos de viaje *trahygoh ahlgoonohs rehkwehrdohs deh byahheh*
These are personal effects	Estos son artículos personales *ehstohs sohn ahrteekoolohs pehrsohnahlehs*
These are not new	Estas cosas no son nuevas *ehstahs kohsahs noh sohn nwehbahs*

Here's the receipt	Aquí está el recibo *ahkee ehstah ehl rehseeboh*
This is for private use	Esto es para uso personal *ehstoh ehs pahrah oosoh pehrsohnahl*
How much import duty do I have to pay?	¿Cuánto tengo que pagar por derechos de aduana? *kwahntoh tehngoh keh pahgahr pohr dehrehchohs deh ahdwahnah?*
Can I go now?	¿Puedo seguir? *pwehdoh sehgheer?*

5.3 Luggage

Porter!	¡Mozo! *mohsoh!*
Could you take this luggage to...?	¿Podría llevar este equipaje a...? *pohdreeah lyehbahr ehsteh ehkeepahheh ah...?*
How much do I owe you?	¿Cuánto le debo? *kwahntoh leh dehboh?*
Where can I find a luggage trolley?	¿Dónde hay carritos para el equipaje? *dohndeh ay kahrreetohs pahrah ehl ehkeepahheh?*
Could you store this luggage for me?	¿Podría dejar este equipaje en la consigna? *pohdreeah dehhahr ehsteh ehkeepahheh ehn lah kohnseegnah?*
Where are the luggage lockers?	¿Dónde está la consigna automática? *dohndeh ehstah lah kohnseegnah ahootohmahteekah?*
I can't get the locker open	No logro abrir la puerta de la consigna *noh lohgroh ahbreer lah pwehrtah deh lah kohnseegnah*
How much is it per item per day?	¿Cuánto sale por bulto y por día? *kwahntoh sahleh pohr booltoh ee pohr deeah?*
This is not my bag/suitcase	Este/ésta no es mi bolso/mi maleta *ehsteh/ehstah noh ehs mee bohlsoh/mee mahlehtah*
There's one item/bag/suitcase missing still	Todavía falta un bulto/un bolso/una maleta *tohdahbeeah fahltah oon booltoh/oon bohlsoh/oonah mahlehtah*
My suitcase is damaged	Me han dañado la maleta/valija *meh ahn dahnyahdoh lah mahlehtah/bahleehah*

5.4 Traffic signs

a la derecha
right
a la izquierda
left
abierto
open
altura máxima
maximum height
arcenes sin afirmar
soft verges
¡atención, peligro!
danger
autopista de peaje
toll road
autovía
motorway
bajada peligrosa
steep hill
calzada resbaladiza
slippery road
cambio de sentido
change of direction
cañada
animals crossing
carretera comarcal
secondary road
carretera cortada
road closed
carretera en mal estado
irregular road surface
carretera nacional
main road
ceda el paso
give way
cerrado
closed
cruce peligroso
dangerous crossing
curvas en ... km
bends for...km
despacio
drive slowly
desprendimientos
loose rocks
desvío
diversion
dirección prohibida
no entry
dirección única
one-way traffic
encender las luces
switch on lights
espere
wait
estacionamiento reglamentado
limited parking zone
excepto...
except for...
fin de...
end of...
hielo
ice on road
niebla
beware fog
obras
roadworks ahead
paso a nivel (sin barreras)
level crossing (no gates)
paso de ganado
cattle crossing
peaje
toll
peatones
pedestrian crossing
precaución
caution
prohibido estacionar
no parking
prohibido adelantar/rebasar
no overtaking
puesto de socorro
first aid
salida
exit
salida de camiones
factory/works exit
substancias peligrosas
dangerous substances
travesía peligrosa
dangerous crossing
zona peatonal
pedestrian zone

5.5 The car

See the diagram on page 51.

5.6 The petrol station

How many kilometres to the next petrol station, please? — ¿Cuántos kilómetros faltan para la próxima gasolinera?
kwahntohs keelohmehtrohs fahltahn pahrah lah prohxeemah gahsohleenehrah?

I would like...litres of..., please — Póngame...litros de..., por favor
pohngahmeh...leetrohs deh..., pohr fahbohr

– super — Póngame...litros de gasolina súper
pohngahmeh...leetrohs de gahsohleenah soopehr

– leaded — Póngame...litros de gasolina normal
pohngahmeh...leetrohs deh gahsohleenah nohrmahl

– unleaded	Póngame...litros de gasolina sin plomo *pohngahmeh...leetrohs deh gahsohleenah seen plohmoh*
– diesel	Póngame...litros de gasóleo *pohngahmeh...leetrohs deh gahsohlehoh*
I would like... worth of petrol, please	Póngame gasolina por... *pohngahmeh gahsohleenah pohr...*
Fill her up, please	Lléneme el depósito/tanque, por favor *lyehnehmeh ehl dehpohseetoh/tahnkeh, pohr fahbohr*
Could you check...?	¿Podría controlar/revisar...? *pohdreeah kohntrohlahr/rehbeesar?*
– the oil level	¿Podría controlar/revisar el nivel del aceite? *pohdreeah kohntrohlahr/rehbeesar ehl neebehl dehl ahseheeteh?*
– the tyre pressure	¿Podría controlar/revisar la presión de los neumáticos? *pohdreeah kohntrohlahr/rehbeesar lah prehsyohn deh lohs nehoomahteekohs?*
Could you change the oil, please?	¿Podría cambiar el aceite? *pohdreeah kahmbyahr ehl ahseheeteh?*
Could you clean the windows/the windscreen, please?	¿Podría limpiar los cristales/el parabrisas? *pohdreeah leempyahr lohs kreestahlehs/ehl pahrahbreesahs?*
Could you give the car a wash, please?	¿Podría lavar el carro/auto/coche? *pohdreeah lahbahr ehl kahrroh/ahootoh/kohcheh?*

5.7 Breakdown and repairs

I'm having car trouble. Could you give me a hand?	Tengo una avería. ¿Podría ayudarme? *tehngoh oonah ahbehreeah. pohdreeah ahyoodahrmeh?*
I've run out of petrol	Me quedé sin gasolina/bencina/nafta *meh kehdeh seen gahsohleenah/behnseenah/nahftah*
I've locked the keys in the car	Me he dejado las llaves en el carro/auto/coche *meh eh dehhahdoh lahs lyabehs ehn ehl kahrroh/ahootoh/kohcheh*
The car/motorbike/moped won't start	El carro/coche/la moto/el ciclomotor no arranca *ehl kahrroh/kohcheh/lah mohtoh/ehl seeklohmohtohr noh ahrrahnkah*
Could you contact the recovery service for me, please?	¿Podría avisar al auxilio en carretera? *pohdreeah ahbeesar ahl ahooxeelyoh ehn kahrrehtehrah?*
Could you call a garage for me, please?	¿Podría llamar por teléfono a un taller mecánico? *pohdreeah lyahmahr pohr tehlehfohnoh ah oon tahlyehr mehkahneekoh?*
Could you give me a lift to...?	¿Me podría llevar a...? *meh pohdreeah lyehbahr ah...?*

– a garage/into town?	¿Me podría llevar a un taller mecánico/a la ciudad? *meh pohdreeah lyehbahr ah oon tahlyehr mehkahneekoh/ah lah syoodahdh?*
– a phone booth?	¿Me podría llevar a una caseta/cabina de teléfonos? *meh pohdreeah lyehbahr ah oonah kahsehtah/ kahbeenah deh tehlehfohnohs?*
– an emergency phone?	¿Me podría llevar a un teléfono de emergencia? *meh pohdreeah lyehbahr ah oon tehlehfohnoh deh ehmehrhehnsyah?*
Can we take my bicycle/moped?	¿Podríamos llevar la bicicleta/el ciclomotor? *pohdreeahmohs lyehbahr lah beeseeklehtah/ehl seeklohmohtohr?*
Could you tow me to a garage?	¿Podría remolcarme hasta un taller mecánico? *pohdreeah rehmohlkahrmeh ahstah oon tahlyehr mehkahneekoh?*
There's probably something wrong with...(See 5.8).	Me parece que está fallando el/la... *meh pahrehseh keh ehstah fahlyahndoh ehl/lah...*
Can you fix it?	¿Podría arreglarlo? *pohdreeah ahrrehglahrloh?*
Could you fix my tyre?	¿Podría arreglar el neumático? *pohdreeah ahrrehglahr ehl nehoomahteekoh?*
Could you change this wheel?	¿Podría cambiar esta rueda? *pohdreeah kahmbyahr ehstah rwehdah?*
Can you fix it so it'll get me to...?	¿Podría arreglarlo de tal manera que pueda seguir hasta...? *pohdreeah ahrrehglahrloh deh tahl mahnehrah keh pwehdah sehgheer ahstah...?*
Which garage can help me?	¿En qué taller me podrán ayudar entonces? *ehn keh tahlyehr meh pohdrahn ahyoodahr ehntohnsehs?*
When will my car/bicycle be ready?	¿Para cuándo estará mi coche/bicicleta? *pahrah kwahndoh ehstahrah mee kohcheh/beeseeklehtah?*
Can I wait for it here?	¿Puedo esperar aquí? *pwehdoh ehspehrahr ahkee?*
How much will it cost?	¿Cuánto me va a salir? *kwahntoh meh bah ah sahleer?*
Could you itemise the bill?	¿Podría especificar la cuenta? *pohdreeah ehspehseefeekahr lah kwehntah?*
Can I have a receipt for the insurance?	¿Me podría dar un recibo para el seguro? *meh pohdreeah dahr oon rehseeboh pahrah ehl sehgooroh?*

The parts of a car

(the diagram shows the numbered parts)

1 battery	la batería	*lah bahtehreeah*
2 rear light	el faro piloto	*ehl fahroh peelohtoh*
3 rear-view mirror	el retrovisor	*ehl rehtrohbeesohr*
reversing light	la luz de marcha atrás	*lah loos deh mahrchah ahtrahs*
4 aerial	la antena	*lah ahntehnah*
car radio	la autorradio	*lah ahootohrrahdyoh*
5 petrol tank	el depósito/tanque de gasolina	*ehl dehpohseetoh/tahnkeh deh gahsohleenah*
inside mirror	el espejo interior	*ehl ehspehhoh eentehreeohr*
6 sparking plugs	las bujías	*lahs booheeahs*
fuel filter/pump	el separador de gasolina	*ehl sehpahrahdohr deh gahsohleenah*
7 wing mirror	el espejo exterior	*ehl ehspehoh ehxtehryohr*
8 bumper	el parachoques	*ehl pahrahchohkehs*
carburettor	el carburador	*ehl kahrboorahdohr*
crankcase	el cárter	*ehl kahrtehr*
cylinder	el cilindro	*ehl seeleendroh*
ignition	los contactos del ruptor	*lohs kohntahktohs dehl rooptohr*
warning light	la luz piloto	*lah loos peelohtoh*
dynamo	la dinamo	*lah deenahmoh*
accelerator	el pedal del acelerador	*ehl pehdahl dehl ahsehlehrahdohr*
handbrake	el freno de mano	*ehl frehnoh deh mahnoh*
valve	la válvula	*lah bahlboolah*
9 silencer	el silenciador	*ehl seelehnsyahdohr*
10 boot	el maletero/la cajuela	*ehl mahlehtehroh* *lah kahhwehlah*
11 headlight	el faro	*ehl fahroh*
crank shaft	el cigueñal	*ehl seegwehnyahl*
12 air filter	el filtro de aire	*ehl feeltroh deh ayreh*
fog lamp	la luz antiniebla trasera	*lah loos ahnteenyehblah trahsehrah*
13 engine block	el bloque motor	*ehl blohkeh mohtohr*
camshaft	el árbol de levas	*ehl ahrbohl deh lehbahs*
oil filter/pump	el filtro de aceite	*ehl feeltroh deh ahseheeteh*
dipstick	la varilla indicadora de nivel de aceite	*lah bahreelyah eendeekahdohrah deh neebehl deh ahseyteh*
pedal	el pedal	*ehl pehdahl*
14 door	la puerta	*lah pwertah*
15 radiator	el radiador	*ehl rahdyahdohr*
16 brake disc	el disco del freno	*ehl deeskoh dehl frehnoh*
spare wheel	la rueda de auxilio	*lah rwehdah deh ahookseeleeoh*
17 indicator	el intermitente	*ehl eentehrmeetehnteh*
steering wheel	el volante	*ehl bohlahnteh*
18 windscreen wiper	el limpiaparabrisas	*ehl leempyahpahrahbreesahs*
19 shock absorbers	los amortiguadores	*lohs ahmohrteegwahdohrehs*
sunroof	el techo corredizo	*ehl tehchoh kohrrehdeesoh*
spoiler	el spoiler	*ehl spoheelehr*

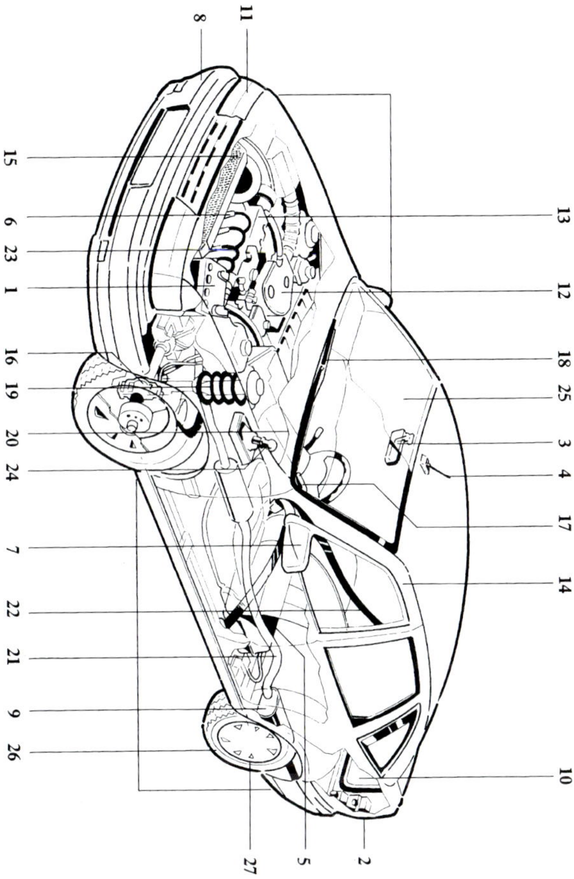

	starter motor	el motor de arranque	*ehl mohtohr deh ahrrahnkeh*
20	steering column	el cárter de la dirección	*ehl kahrtehr deh lah deerehksyohn*
21	exhaust pipe	el tubo de escape	*ehl tooboh deh ehskahpeh*
22	seat belt	el cinturón de seguridad	*ehl seentoorohn deh sehgooreedahdh*
	fan	el ventilador	*ehl behnteelahdohr*
23	distributor cables	los cables del distribuidor	*lohs kahblehs dehl deestreebooeedohr*
24	gear lever	la palanca de cambios/velocidades	*lah pahlahnkah deh kahmbyohs/behlohseedahdes*
25	windscreen	el parabrisas	*ehl pahrahbreesahs*
	water pump	la bomba de agua	*lah bohmbah deh ahgwah*
26	wheel	la rueda	*lah rwehdah*
27	hubcap	el tapacubos	*ehl tahpahkoobohs*
	piston	el émbolo/pistón	*ehl ehmbohloh/peestohn*

5.8 The bicycle/moped

See the diagram on page 55.

- **Cycle paths** are rare in Latin American countries.

No tengo piezas de repuesto para su coche/su bicicleta	I don't have parts for your car/bicycle
Las piezas de repuesto me las tienen que traer de otro sitio	I have to get the parts from somewhere else
Tengo que encargar las piezas de repuesto	I have to order the parts
Eso llevará medio día	That'll take half a day
Eso llevará un día	That'll take a day
Eso llevará unos días	That'll take a few days
Eso llevará una semana	That'll take a week
Su coche ha quedado totalmente destruido	Your car is a write-off
Ya no se puede hacer nada para arreglarlo	It can't be repaired
El coche/la moto/el ciclomotor/la bicicleta estará para las...	The car/motorbike/moped/ bicycle will be ready at... o'clock

5.9 Renting a vehicle

I'd like to rent a...	Quisiera alquilar un/una... *keesyehrah ahlkeelahr oon/oonah...*
Do I need a (special) licence for that?	¿Hace falta un permiso de conducir (especial)? *ahseh fahltah oon pehrmeesoh deh kohndooseer (ehspehsyahl)?*
I'd like to rent the...for...	Quisiera alquilar el/la...por... *keesyehrah ahlkeelahr ehl/lah...pohr...*
– one day	Quisiera alquilar el/la...por un día *keesyehrah ahlkeelahr ehl/lah...pohr oon deeah*
– two days	Quisiera alquilar el/la...por dos días *keesyehrah ahlkeelahr ehl/lah...pohr dohs deeahs*
How much is that per day/week?	¿Cuánto sale por día/semana? *kwahntoh sahleh pohr deeah/pohr sehmahnah?*
How much is the deposit?	¿Cuánto es la fianza? *kwahntoh ehs lah fyahnsah?*
Could I have a receipt for the deposit?	¿Me podría dar un recibo por el pago de la fianza? *meh pohdreeah dahr oon rehseeboh pohr ehl pahgoh deh lah fyahnsah?*
How much is the surcharge per kilometre?	¿Cuánto hay que pagar extra por kilómetro? *kwahntoh ay keh pahgahr ehxtrah pohr keelohmehtroh?*
Does that include petrol?	¿Está incluida la gasolina? *ehstah eenklooeedah lah gahsohleenah?*

Does that include insurance?	¿Está incluido el seguro? *ehstah eenklooeedoh ehl sehgooroh?*
What time can I pick the...up tomorrow?	¿A qué hora puedo pasar mañana a buscar el/la...? *ah keh ohrah pwehdoh pahsahr mahnyahnah ah booskahr ehl/lah...?*
When does the...have to be back?	¿A qué hora tengo que devolver el/la...? *ah keh ohrah tehngoh keh dehbohlbehr ehl/lah...?*
Where's the petrol tank?	¿Dónde está el depósito/tanque de gasolina? *dohndeh ehstah ehl dehpohseetoh/tahnkeh deh gahsohleenah?*
What sort of fuel does it take?	¿Qué tipo de combustible hay que echarle? *keh teepoh deh kohmboosteebleh ay keh ehchahrleh?*

5.10 Hitchhiking

Where are you heading?	¿Adónde va? *ahdohndeh bah?*
Can I come along?	¿Me podría llevar? *meh pohdreeah lyehbahr?*
Can my boyfriend/ girlfriend come too?	¿Podría llevar también a mi amigo/amiga? *pohdreeah lyehbahr tahmbyehn ah mee ahmeegoh/ahmeegah?*
I'm trying to get to...	Voy a... *boy ah...*
Is that on the way to...?	¿Eso está camino de...? *ehsoh ehstah kahmeenoh deh...?*
Could you drop me off...?	¿Me podría dejar...? *meh pohdreeah dehhahr...?*
– here?	¿Me podría dejar aquí mismo? *meh pohdreeah dehhahr ahkee meesmoh?*
– at the...exit?	¿Me podría dejar en la salida de...? *meh pohdreeah dehhahr ehn lah sahleedah deh...?*
– in the centre?	¿Me podría dejar en el centro? *meh pohdreeah dehhahr ehn ehl sehntroh?*
– at the next roundabout?	¿Me podría dejar en la próxima rotonda/glorieta? *meh pohdreeah dehhahr ehn lah prohxeemah rohtohndah/glohryehtah?*
Could you stop here, please?	¿Podría pararse aquí? *pohdreeah pahrahrseh ahkee?*
I'd like to get out here	Quisiera bajarme aquí *keesyehrah bahhahrmeh ahkee*
Thanks for the lift	Gracias por llevarme *grahsyahs pohr lyehbahrmeh*

The parts of a bicycle

(the diagram shows the numbered parts)

1	rear lamp	el piloto	*ehl peelohtoh*
2	rear wheel	la rueda trasera	*lah rwehdah trahsehrah*
3	(luggage) carrier	el portaequipajes	*ehl pohrtahehkeepahhehs*
4	bicycle fork	la cabeza	*lah kahbehsah*
5	bell	el timbre	*ehl teembreh*
	inner tube	la cámara	*lah kahmahrah*
	tyre	el neumático/la cubierta	*ehl nehoomahteekoh/lah koobyehrtah*
6	crank	la biela	*lah byehlah*
7	gear change	el cambio de velocidades	*ehl kahmbyoh deh behloseedahdehs*
	wire	el hilo	*ehl eeloh*
	dynamo	la dinamo	*lah deenahmoh*
	bicycle trailer	el remolque de bicicleta	*ehl rehmohlkeh deh beeseeklehtah*
	frame	el cuadro	*ehl kwahdroh*
8	dress guard	el guardafaldas	*ehl gwardahfahldahs*
9	chain	la cadena de rodillos	*lah kahdehnah deh rohdeelyohs*
	chain guard	el cubrecadena/el cárter	*ehl koobrehkahdehnah/ehl kahrtehr*
	chain lock	la cadena antirrobo	*lah kahdehnah ahnteerrohboh*
	milometer	el contador kilométrico	*ehl kohntahdohr keelohmehtreekoh*
	child's seat	la silla para niños	*lah seelyah pahrah neenyohs*
10	headlamp	el faro	*ehl fahroh*
	bulb	la bombilla	*lah bohmbeelyah*
11	pedal	el pedal	*ehl pehdahl*
12	pump	la bombilla	*lah bohmbeelyah*
13	reflector	el cristal reflectante	*ehl kreestahl rehflehktahnteh*
14	brake pad	la zapatilla del freno	*lah thahpahteelyah dehl frehnoh*
15	brake cable	el cable del freno	*ehl kahbleh dehl frehnoh*
16	ring lock	la cerradura	*lah sehrrahdoorah*
17	carrier straps	las bandas elásticas	*lahs bahndahs ehlahsteekahs*
	tachometer		
18	spoke	el velocímetro	*ehl behlohseemehtroh*
19	mudguard	el radio/el rayo	*ehl rahdyoh/ehl rahyoh*
20	handlebar	el guardabarros	*ehl gwahrdahbahrrohs*
21	chain wheel	el manillar	*ehl mahneelyahr*
	toe clip	el piñón	*ehl peenyohn*
22	crank axle	el calapiés	*ehl kahlahpyehs*
	drum brake	el eje del cigueñal	*ehl ehhe dehl seegwehnyal*
	rim	el freno de tambor	*ehl frehnoh deh tahmbohr*
23	tube	la llanta	*lah lyahntah*
24	valve	la válvula	*lah bahlboolah*
	valve tube	el tubo de la válvula	*ehl tooboh deh lah bahlboolah*

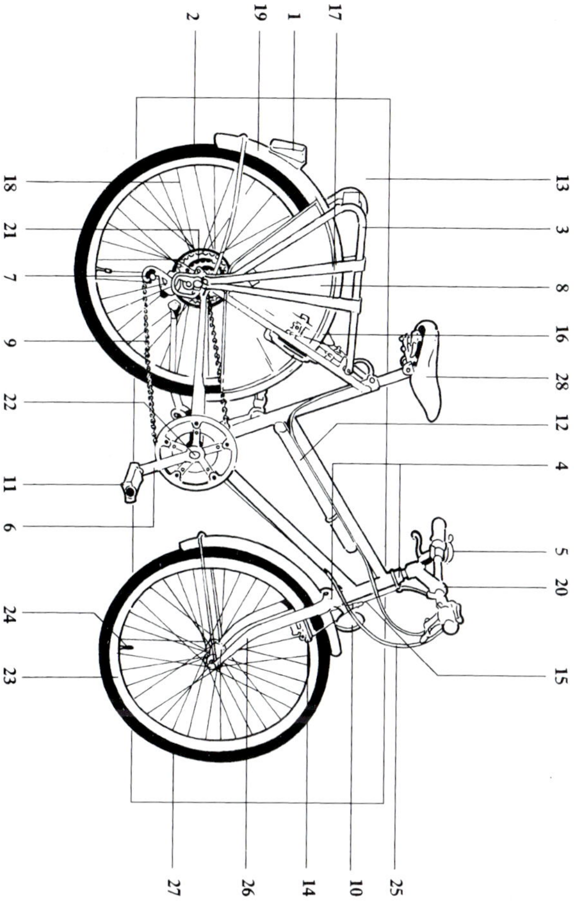

25 gear cable	el cable de velocidades	*ehl kahbleh deh behlohseedahdehs*
26 fork	la horquilla	*lah ohrkeelyah*
27 front wheel	la rueda delantera	*lah rwehdah dehlahntehrah*
28 seat	la silla	*la seelyah*

6

Public transport

6 Public transport

6.1 In general

● **In general,** rail travel in Latin American countries is cheaper than buses, but slower and less comfortable. In countries where the rail network to remote areas has not been updated, the visitor has to rely on buses for land transportation, or on air services.

Announcements

El tren [de las 10:40] con destino a..., ..., saldrá con (unos)...minutos de retraso	The [10:40] train to...has been delayed by 15 minutes
Por la vía 5 entrará el tren [de las 10:40] con destino a.../ procedente de...	The train now arriving at platform 5 is the [10:40] train to .../from...
En la vía 5 está por partir el tren [de las 10:40]...	The [10:40] train to...is about to leave from platform 5
Su atención, por favor Manténganse lejos de la via; un tren rápido pasará por la plataforma...	Attention please! Keep your distance from the rail track, an express train will pass on platform...
Nos estamos aproximando a la estación de...	We're now approaching...

Where does this train go to?	¿Adónde va este tren? *ahdohndeh bah ehsteh trehn?*
Does this boat go to...?	¿Este barco va a...? *ehsteh bahrkoh bah ah...?*
Can I take this bus to...?	¿Puedo tomar este omnibús/autobús/ camión para ir a...? *pwehdoh tohmahr ehsteh ohmneeboos/ ahootohboos/kahmeeohn pahrah eer ah...?*
Does this train stop at...?	¿Este tren para en...? *ehsteh trehn pahrah ehn...?*
Is this seat taken/free /reserved?	¿Está ocupado/libre/reservado este asiento? *ehstah ohkoopahdoh/leebreh/rehsehrbahdoh ehsteh ahsyehntoh?*
I've booked...	He reservado... *eh rehsehrbahdoh...*
Could you tell me where I have to get off for... ?	¿Me podría decir dónde me tengo que bajar para ir a...? *meh pohdreeah dehseer dohndeh meh tehngoh keh bah<u>h</u>ar pahrah eer ah...?*
Could you let me know when we get to...?	¿Me podría avisar cuando lleguemos a...? *meh pohdreeah ahbeesahr kwahndoh lyehghehmohs ah...?*
Could you stop at the next stop, please?	La próxima parada, por favor *lah prohxeemah pahrahdah pohr fahbohr*

Where are we now?	¿Dónde estamos? *dohndeh ehstahmohs?*
Do I have to get off here?	¿Tengo que bajarme aquí? *tehngoh keh bahhahrmeh ahkee?*
Have we already passed...?	¿Ya hemos pasado...? *yah ehmohs pahsahdoh...?*
How long have I been asleep?	¿Cuánto tiempo he dormido? *kwahntoh tyehmpoh eh dohrmeedoh?*
How long does... stop here?	¿Cuánto tiempo se queda aquí...? *kwahntoh tyehmpoh seh kehdah ahkee?*
Can I come back on the same ticket?	¿Este boleto me sirve para volver? *ehsteh bohlehtoh meh seerbeh pahrah bohlbehr?*
Can I change on this ticket?	¿Se puede hacer trasbordo con este boleto? *seh pwehdeh ahthehr trahsbohrdoh kohn ehsteh bohlehtoh?*
How long is this ticket valid for?	¿Hasta cuándo es válido este boleto? *ahstah kwahndoh ehs bahleedoh ehsteh bohlehtoh*

6.2 Questions to passengers

Ticket types

¿Primera o segunda clase?	First or second class?
¿Boleto de ida o de ida y vuelta?	Single or return?
¿Fumadores o no fumadores?	Smoking or non-smoking?
¿Ventanilla o pasillo?	Window or aisle?
¿Adelante o atrás?	Front or back?
¿Asiento o litera?	Seat or couchette?
¿Arriba, en el medio o abajo?	Top, middle or bottom?
¿Clase turista o preferente?	Tourist class or business class?
¿Camarin o butaca?	Cabin or seat?
¿Individual o doble?	Single or double?
¿Cuántas personas viajan?	How many are travelling?

Destination

¿Adónde quiere ir?	Where are you travelling?
¿Qué día sale?	When are you leaving?
Su...sale a las...	Your...leaves at...
Tiene que hacer trasbordo	You have to change trains
Tiene que bajarse en...	You have to get off at...
Tiene que pasar por...	You have to travel via...
El viaje de ida es el día...	The outward journey is on...
El viaje de vuelta es el día...	The return journey is on...
Tiene que embarcar a las...a más tardar	You have to be on board by...

Boletos, por favor	Your ticket, please
Su reserva/reservación, por favor	Your reservation, please
Su pasaporte, por favor	Your passport, please
Se ha equivocado de asiento	You're in the wrong seat
Se ha equivocado de...	You're on/in the wrong...
Este asiento está reservado	This seat is reserved
Tiene que pagar un suplemento	You'll have to pay a supplement
El...tiene un retraso de...minutos	The...has been delayed by...minutes

6.3 Tickets

Where can I...?	¿Dónde...? *dohndeh...?*
– buy a ticket?	¿Dónde se compran los boletos? *dohndeh seh kohmprahn lohs bohlehtohs?*
– make a reservation?	¿Dónde se hacen las reservas/ reservaciones? *dohndeh seh ahsehn lahs rehsehrbahs/ rehsehrbahsyohnes?*
– book a flight?	¿Dónde puedo hacer una reserva para un vuelo? *dohndeh pwehdoh ahsehr oonah rehsehrbah pahrah oon bwehloh?*
Could I have a...to..., please?	Quiero un/una...a... *kyehroh oon/oonah...ah...*
– a single	Quiero un boleto de ida a... *kyehroh oon bohlehtoh deh eedah ah...*
– a return	Quiero un boleto de ida y vuelta a... *kyehroh oon bohlehtoh deh eedah ee bwehltah ah...*
first class	en primera clase *ehn preemehrah klahseh*
second class	en segunda clase *ehn sehgoondah klahseh*
tourist class	en clase turista *ehn klahseh tooreestah*
business class	en clase preferente *ehn klahseh prehfehrehnteh*
I'd like to book a seat/couchette/cabin	Quisiera reservar un asiento/una litera/un camarín *keesyehrah rehsehrbahr oon ahsyehntoh/ oonah leetehrah/oon kahmahreen*
I'd like to book a berth in the sleeping car	Quisiera reservar un camarín/una alcoba en un coche cama *keesyehrah rehsehrbahr oon kahmahreen/ oonah ahlkohbah ehn oon kohcheh kahmah*
top/middle/bottom	arriba/en el medio/abajo *ahrreebah/ehn ehl mehdyoh/ahbahhoh*
smoking/no smoking	fumadores/no fumadores *foomahdohrehs/noh foomahdohrehs*

6 Public transport

by the window	ventanilla *behntahneelyah*
single/double	individual/doble *eendeebeedwahl/dohbleh*
at the front/back	adelante/atrás *ahdehlahnteh/ahtrahs*
There are...of us	Somos...personas *sohmohs...pehrsohnahs*
a car	un carro/auto *oon kahrroh/ahootoh*
a caravan	una caravana/casa rodante *oonah kahrahbahnah/kahsah rohdahnteh*
...bicycles	...bicicletas *...beeseeklehtahs*
Do you also have...?	¿Tienen...? *tyehnehn...?*
– season tickets?	¿Tienen abonos? *tyehnen ahbohnohs?*
– weekly tickets?	¿Tienen abonos semanales? *tyehnehn ahbohnohs sehmahnahlehs?*
– monthly season tickets?	¿Tienen abonos mensuales? *tyehnehn ahbohnohs mehnswahlehs?*

6.4 Information

Where's...?	¿Dónde hay...? *dohndeh ay...?*
Where's the information desk?	¿Dónde está la oficina de información? *dohndeh ehstah lah ohfeeseenah deh eenfohrmahsyohn?*
Where can I find a timetable?	¿Dónde hay un horario? *dohndeh ay oon ohrahryoh?*
Where's the...desk?	¿Dónde está el mostrador de...? *dohndeh ehstah ehl mohstrahdohr deh...?*
Do you have a city map with the bus/the underground routes on it?	¿Tendría un plano de la ciudad con la red de autobuses/metro? *tehndreeah oon plahnoh deh lah syoodahdh kohn lah rehdh deh ahootohboosehs/ mehtroh?*
Do you have a timetable?	¿Tendría un horario? *tehndreeah oon ohrahryoh?*
I'd like to confirm/ cancel/change my booking for/trip to...	Quisiera confirmar/cancelar/cambiar mi reserva/mi viaje a... *keesyehrah kohnfeermahr/kahnsehlahr/ kahmbyahr mee rehsehrbah/mee byahheh ah...*
Will I get my money back?	¿Me devuelven el dinero? *meh dehbwehlbehn ehl deenehroh?*
I want to go to... How do I get there? (What's the quickest way there?)	Tengo que ir a...¿Cómo hago para llegar (lo más rápido posible)? *tehngoh keh eer ah...kohmoh ahgoh pahrah lyehgahr(loh mahs rahpeedoh pohseebleh)?*
How much is a single/return to...?	¿Cuánto vale un boleto de ida/de ida y vuelta a...? *kwahntoh bahleh oon bohlehtoh deh eedah ee bwehltah ah...?*

Do I have to pay a supplement?	¿Tengo que pagar algún suplemento?	*tehngoh keh pahgahr ahlgoon sooplehmehntoh?*
Can I interrupt my journey with this ticket?	¿Con este boleto puedo hacer una parada intermedia?	*kohn ehsteh bohlehtoh pwehdoh ahthehr oonah pahrahdah eentehrmehdyah?*
How much luggage am I allowed?	¿Cuánto equipaje puedo llevar?	*kwahntoh ehkeepahheh pwehdoh lyebahr?*
Can I send my luggage in advance?	¿Puedo enviar mi equipaje por anticipado?	*pwehdoh ehnbeeahr mee ehkeepahheh pohr ahnteeseepahdoh?*
Does this...travel direct?	¿Este...va directo?	*ehsteh...bah deerehktoh?*
Do I have to change? Where?	¿Tengo que hacer trasbordo? ¿Dónde?	*tehngoh keh ahthehr trahsbohrdoh? dohndeh?*
Will there be any stopovers?	¿Habrá escalas?	*ahbrah ehskahlahs?*
Does the boat call in at any ports on the way?	¿El barco hace alguna escala?	*ehl bahrkoh ahseh ahlgoonah ehskahlah?*
Does the train/ bus stop at...?	¿Este tren/este autobús para en...?	*ehsteh trehn/ehsteh ahootohboos pahrah ehn...?*
Where should I get off?	¿Dónde me tengo que bajar?	*dohndeh meh tehngoh keh bahhahr?*
Is there a connection to...?	¿Hay enlace para...?	*ay ehnlahseh pahrah...?*
How long do I have to wait?	¿Cuánto tengo que esperar?	*kwahntoh tehngoh keh ehspehrahr?*
When does...leave?	¿Cuándo sale...?	*kwahndoh sahleh...?*
What time does the first/next/last...leave?	¿A qué hora sale el primer/próximo/último...?	*ah keh ohrah sahleh ehl preemehr/prohxeemoh/oolteemoh...?*
How long does...take?	¿Cuánto tarda...en llegar?	*kwahntoh tahrdah...ehn lyehgahr?*
What time does...arrive in...?	¿A qué hora llega...a...?	*ah keh ohrah lyegah...ah...?*
Where does the...to... leave from?	¿De dónde sale el...a...?	*deh dohndeh sahleh ehl...ah...?*
Is this...to...?	¿Este es...a...?	*ehsteh ehs...ah...?*

6.5 Aeroplanes

● **On arrival** at an airport in Spanish speaking countries, you will find the following signs:

llegadas arrivals	salidas departures

6.6 Trains

● **In some countries** first and second class are available, and even sleeping berths for long distance train services. In others, local trains servicing urban areas are the fastest and most reliable public transportation, along with modern underground networks.

6.7 Taxis

● **There are plenty of taxis** in most cities. Supplements are payable for luggage and travel to stations or airports. It is advisable to inquire about the price in advance and make sure that you are hiring a city taxi.

libre	ocupado	parada de taxis
for hire	booked	taxi rank

Taxi!	¡Taxi! *tahxee!*
Could you get me a taxi, please?	¿Me podría llamar un taxi? *meh pohdreeah lyahmahr oon tahksee?*
Where can I find a taxi around here?	¿Dónde se puede tomar un taxi por aquí? *dohndeh seh pwehdeh tohmahr oon tahxee pohr ahkee?*
Could you take me to..., please?	A..., por favor *ah..., pohr fahbohr*
– this address	A esta dirección, por favor *ah ehstah deerehksyohn, pohr fahbohr*
– the...hotel	Al hotel..., por favor *ahl ohtehl..., pohr fahbohr*
– the town/city centre	Al centro, por favor *ahl sehntroh, pohr fahbohr*
– the station	A la estación, por favor *ah lah ehstahsyohn, pohr fahbohr*
– the airport	Al aeropuerto, por favor *ahl ahehrohpwehrtoh, pohr fahbohr*
How much is the trip to...?	¿Cuánto sale el recorrido hasta...? *kwahntoh sahleh ehl rehkohrreedoh ahstah...?*
How far is it to...?	¿Cuánto es hasta...? *kwahntoh ehs ahstah...?*
Could you turn on the meter, please?	¿Podría poner en marcha el taxímetro? *pohdreeah pohnehr ehn mahrchah ehl tahxeemehtroh?*
I'm in a hurry	Estoy apurado *ehstoy ahpoorahdoh*
Could you speed up/slow down a little?	¿Podría ir más rápido/más despacio? *pohdreeah eer mahs rahpeedoh/mahs dehspasyoh?*
Could you take a different route?	¿Podría ir por otro camino? *pohdreeah eer pohr ohtroh kahmeenoh?*
I'd like to get out here, please	Déjeme aquí *dehhehmeh ahkee*

You have to go...here	Siga...aquí *seegah...ahkee*
You have to go straight on here	Siga derecho aquí *seegah dehrehchoh akee*
You have to turn left here	Doble a la izquierda aquí *dohbleh ah lah eeskyehrdah ahkee*
You have to turn right here	Doble a la derecha aquí *dohbleh ah lah dehrehchah ahkee*
This is it	Es aquí *ehs ahkee*
Could you wait a minute for me, please?	Espéreme un momentito/tantito, por favor *ehspehrehmeh oon mohmehnteetoh/ tahnteetoh, pohr fahbohr*

7 Overnight accommodation

7 Overnight accommodation

7.1 General

● **In most of the** Latin American countries, cheap hotels are located around train and bus stations, while expensive international hotels can be found in the centre of large cities, near airports or in residential districts. Tourist resorts normally offer a good variety of overnight accommodation.

¿Cuánto tiempo piensa quedarse?	How long will you be staying?
Rellene este formulario, por favor	Fill in this form, please
¿Me permite su pasaporte?	Could I see your passport?
Tiene que pagar una fianza	I'll need a deposit
Tiene que pagar por adelantado	You'll have to pay in advance

My name's...I've made a reservation over the phone/by mail — Me llamo...Reservé una habitación por teléfono/por carta
meh lyahmoh...eh rehsehrbeh oonah ahbeetahsyohn pohr tehlehfohnoh/pohr kahrtah

How much is it per night/week/month? — ¿Cuánto sale por noche/semana/mes?
kwahntoh sahleh pohr nohcheh/sehmahnah/mehs?

We'll be staying at least...nights/weeks — Pensamos quedarnos al menos...noches/semanas
pehnsahmohs kehdahrnohs ahl mehnohs...nohchehs/sehmahnahs

We don't know yet — Todavía no lo sabemos exactamente
tohdahbeeah noh loh sahbehmohs ehxahktahmehnteh

Do you allow pets (cats/dogs)? — ¿Están permitidos los animales domésticos (perros/gatos)?
ehstahn pehrmeeteedohs lohs ahneemahlehs dohmehsteekohs (pehrrohs/gahtohs)?

What time does the gate/door open/close? — ¿A qué hora cierran/abren la verja/la puerta de entrada?
ah keh ohrah syehrrahn/ahbrehn lah behrhah/lah pwehrtah deh ehntrahdah?

Could you get me a taxi, please? — ¿Podría llamar un taxi?
pohdreeah lyahmahr oon tahxee?

Is there any mail for me? — ¿Hay carta para mí?
ay kahrtah pahrah mee?

7.2 Camping

See the diagram on page 69.

Puede elegir el sitio usted mismo	You can pick your own site
El sitio se lo asignamos nosotros	You'll be allocated a site
Este es el número de su emplazamiento	This is your site number
Por favor pegue esto en el parabrisas del carro/auto	Stick this on your car, please
No pierda esta tarjeta	Please don't lose this card

Where's the manager?	¿Dónde está el encargado? *dohndeh ehstah ehl ehnkahrgahdoh?*
Are we allowed to camp here?	¿Podemos acampar aquí? *pohdehmohs ahkahmpahr ahkee?*
There are...of us and ...tents	Somos...personas y...tiendas/carpas *sohmohs...pehrsohnahs ee...tyehndahs/ kahrpahs*
Can we pick our own site?	¿Podemos elegir el sitio nosotros mismos? *pohdehmohs ehlehheer ehl seetyoh nohsohtrohs meesmohs?*
Do you have a quiet spot for us?	¿Nos podría dar un sitio tranquilo? *nohs pohdreeah dahr oon seetyoh trahnkeeloh?*
Do you have any other sites available?	¿No tiene otro sitio libre? *noh tyehneh ohtroh seetyoh leebreh?*
It's too windy/sunny/ shady here.	Hay mucho viento/mucho sol/mucha sombra *ay moochoh byehntoh/moochoh sohl/moochah sohmbrah*
It's too crowded here	Hay mucha gente *ay moochah hehnteh*
The ground's too hard/uneven	El suelo es muy duro/muy desigual *ehl swehloh ehs mwee dooroh/mwee dehseegwahl*
Do you have a level spot for the camper/caravan/folding caravan?	¿Tiene un sitio plano para el autocaravana/la caravana/el remolque tienda? *tyehneh oon seetyoh plahnoh pahrah ehl ahootohkahrahbahnah/lah kahrahbahnah/ehl rehmohlkeh-tyehndah?*
Could we have adjoining sites?	¿Tiene dos plazas juntas? *tyehneh dohs plahsahs hoontahs?*
Can we park the car next to the tent?	¿Podemos estacionar el carro/auto/coche junto a la tienda/carpa? *pohdehmohs ehstahsyohnahr ehl karroh/ahootoh/kohcheh hoontoh ah lah tyehndah/kahrpah?*
How much is it per person/tent/caravan/car?	¿Cuánto sale por persona/tienda/caravana/coche? *kwahntoh sahleh pohr pehrsohnah/tyehndah/ kahrahbahnah/kohcheh?*

Are there any...?	¿Hay...? *ay...?*
– any hot showers?	¿Hay duchas con agua caliente? *ay doochahs kohn ahgwah kahlyehnteh?*
– washing machines?	¿Hay lavadoras? *ay lahbahdohrahs?*
Is there a...on the site?	¿En este camping hay...? *ehn ehsteh kahmpeen ay...?*
Is there a children's play area on the site?	¿En este camping hay un sitio para que jueguen los niños? *ehn ehsteh kahmpeen ay oon seetyoh pahrah keh hwehghehn lohs neenyohs?*
Are there covered cooking facilities on the site?	¿En este camping hay un sitio cubierto para cocinar? *ehn ehsteh kahmpeen ay oon seetyoh koobyehrtoh pahrah kohseenahr?*
Can I rent a safe here?	¿Tienen caja fuerte para alquilar? *tyehnehn kahhah fwehrteh pahrah ahlkeelahr?*
Are we allowed to barbecue here?	¿Se pueden hacer barbacoas? *seh pwehdehn ahsehr bahrbahkohahs?*
Are there any power points?	¿Hay tomas de corriente eléctrica? *ay tohmahs deh kohrryehnteh ehlehktreekah?*
Is there drinking water?	¿Hay agua potable? *ay ahgwah pohtahbleh?*
When's the rubbish collected?	¿Cuándo pasan a recoger la basura? *kwahndoh pahsahn ah rehkohhehr lah bahsoorah?*
Do you sell gas bottles (butane gas/propane gas)?	¿Venden bombas de gas (butano/propano)? *behndehn bohmbahs deh gahs(bootahnoh/prohpahnoh)?*

7.3 Hotel/B&B/apartment/holiday house

Do you have a single/double room available?	¿Le queda alguna habitación individual/doble? *leh kehdah ahlgoonah ahbeetahsyohn eendeebeedwahl/dohbleh?*
per person/per room	por persona/por habitación *pohr pehrsohnah/pohr ahbeetahsyohn*
Does that include breakfast/lunch/dinner?	¿Incluye desayuno/comida/cena? *eenklooyeh dehsahyoonoh/kohmeedah/sehnah?*
Could we have two adjoining rooms?	¿Nos puede dar dos habitaciones una al lado de la otra? *nohs pwehdeh dahr dohs ahbeetahsyohnehs oonah ahl lahdoh deh lah ohtrah?*
with/without toilet/bath/shower	con/sin wáter/baño propio/ducha propia *kohn/seen bahtehr prohpyoh/bahnyoh prohpyoh/doochah prohpyah?*
(not) facing the street	que (no) dé a la calle *keh (noh) deh ah lah kahlyeh*
with/without a view of the sea	con/sin vista al mar *kohn/seen beestah ahl mahr*
Is there...in the hotel?	¿El hotel tiene...? *ehl ohtehl tyehneh...?*

Camping equipment

(the diagram shows the numbered parts)

	luggage space	el compartimiento de equipaje	*ehl kohmpahrteemyehntoh de ehkeepahheh*
	can opener	el abrelatas	*ehl ahbrehlahtahs*
	butane gas bottle	la bomba garrafa (de gas butano)	*lah bohmbah gahrrahfah (deh gahs bootahnoh)*
1	pannier	la ciclobolsa	*lah theeklohbohlsah*
2	gas cooker	el hornillo de gas	*ehl ohrneelyoh deh gahs*
3	groundsheet	la lona del suelo	*lah lohnah dehl swehloh*
	mallet	el martillo	*ehl mahrteelyoh*
	hammock	la hamaca	*lah ahmahkah*
4	jerry can	el bidón	*ehl beedohn*
	campfire	la fogata	*lah fohgahtah*
5	folding chair	la silla plegable	*lah seelyah plehgahbleh*
6	insulated picnic box	la bolsa refrigeradora	*lah bohlsah rehfreehehrahdohrah*
	compass	la brújula	*lah broohoolah*
	wick	la mecha	*lah mehchah*
	corkscrew	el sacacorchos	*ehl sahkahkohrchohs*
7	airbed	el colchón neumático	*ehl kohlchohn nehoomahteekoh*
8	airbed plug	el taponcito de la válvula del colchón	*ehl tahpohnseetoh deh lah bahlboolah dehl kohlchohn*
	pump	la bomba neumática	*lah bohmbah nehoomahteekah*
9	awning	el tejadillo	*ehl tehhahdeelyoh*
10	karimat	la esterilla	*lah ehstehreelyah*
11	pan	la olla	*lah ohlyah*
12	pan handle	el mango de la olla	*ehl mahngoh deh lah ohlyah*
	primus stove	el hornillo de querosén	*ehl ohrneelyoh deh kehrohsehn*
	zip	la cremallera	*lah krehmalyehrah*
13	backpack	la mochila	*lah mohcheelah*
14	guy rope	el viento	*ehl byehntoh*
	sleeping bag	el saco de dormir	*ehl sahkoh deh dohrmeer*
15	storm lantern	el farol de tormentas	*ehl fahrohl deh tohrmehntahs*
	camp bed	el catre (de tijera)	*ehl kahtreh (deh teehehrah)*
	table	la mesa	*lah mehsah*
16	tent	la tienda	*lah tyehndah*
17	tent peg	la estaca	*lah ehstakah*
18	tent pole	el palo de tienda	*ehl pahloh deh tyehndah*
	vacuum flask	el termo	*ehl tehrmoh*
19	water bottle	la cantimplora	*lah kahnteemplohrah*
	clothes peg	la pinza	*lah peensah*
	clothes line	la cuerda de tender ropa	*lah kwehrdah deh tehndehr rohpah*
	windbreak	el paravientos/el paraván	*ehl pahrahbyehntohs/ehl pahrahbahn*
20	torch	la linterna de bolsillo	*lah leentehrnah deh bohlseelyoh*
	pocket knife	la navaja	*lah nahbahhah*

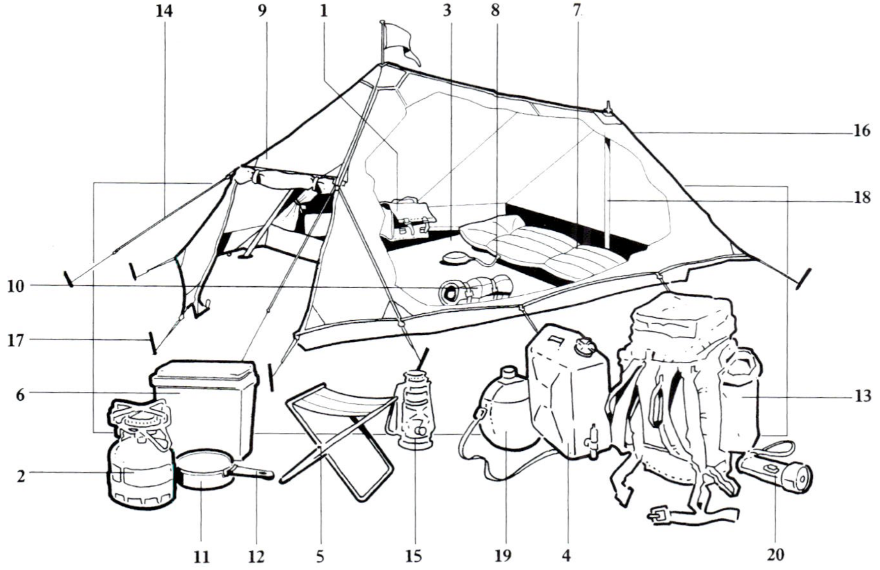
14
9
1
3
8
7
16
18
10
17
6
13
2
11
12
5
15
19
4
20

Is there a lift in the hotel?	¿El hotel tiene ascensor/elevador? *ehl ohtehl tyehneh ahssehnsohr/ ehlehbahdohr?*
Do you have room service?	¿El hotel tiene servicio de habitación? *ehl ohtehl tyehneh sehrbeethyoh deh ahbeetahthyohn?*

Tiene WC y ducha en el mismo piso/en su habitación	You can find the toilet and shower on the same floor/en suite
Por aquí, por favor	This way, please
Su habitación está en el...piso; es la número...	Your room is on the...floor, number...

Could I see the room?	¿Puedo ver la habitación? *pwehdoh behr lah ahbeetahsyohn?*
I'll take this room	Me quedo con esta habitación *meh kehdoh kohn ehstah abeetahsyohn*
We don't like this one	Esta no nos gusta *ehstah noh nohs goostah*
Do you have a larger/ less expensive room?	¿Tiene una habitación más grande/más barata? *tyehneh oonah ahbeetahsyohn mahs grahnde/mahs bahrahtah?*
Could you put in a cot?	¿Puede agregar una cuna? *pwehde ahgrehgahr oonah koonah?*
What time's breakfast?	¿A qué hora es el desayuno? *ah keh ohrah ehs ehl dehsahyoonoh?*
Where's the dining room?	¿Dónde está el comedor? *dohndeh ehstah ehl kohmehdohr?*
Can I have breakfast in my room?	¿Me pueden traer el desayuno a la habitación? *meh pwehdehn trahehr ehl dehsahyoonoh ah lah ahbeetahsyohn?*
Where's the emergency exit/fire escape?	¿Dónde está la salida de emergencia/la escalera de incendios? *dohndeh ehstah lah sahleedah deh ehmehrhehnsyah/lah ehskahlehrah de eensehndyohs?*
Where can I park my car (safely)?	¿Dónde hay un sitio (seguro) para estacionar el carro/auto? *dohndeh ay oon seetyoh sehgooroh pahrah ehstahsyohnahr ehl kahrroh/ahootoh?*
The key to room..., please	La llave de la habitación..., por favor *lah lyahbeh deh lah ahbeetahsyohn..., pohr fahbohr*
Could you put this in the safe, please?	¿Podría dejar esto en la caja fuerte? *pohdreeah dehhahr ehstoh ehn lah cahhah fwehrteh?*
Could you wake me at...tomorrow?	¿Me podría despertar mañana a las...? *meh pohdreeah dehspehrtahr mahnyahnah ah lahs...?*

Could you find a babysitter for me?	¿Me podría conseguir una niñera para el bebé? *meh pohdreeah kohnsehgueer oonah neenyehrah pahrah ehl behbeh?*
Could I have an extra blanket?	¿Tendría una manta extra? *tehndreeah oonah mahntah ehxtrah?*
What days do the cleaners come in?	¿Qué días limpian la habitación? *keh deeahs leempyahn lah ahbeetahsyohn?*
When are the sheets/towels/tea towels changed?	¿Cuándo cambian las sábanas/las toallas/los paños de cocina? *kwahndoh kahmbyahn lahs sahbahnahs/lahs tohahlyahs/lohs pahnyohs deh kohseenah?*

7.4 Complaints

We can't sleep for the noise	No podemos dormir por el ruido *noh pohdehmohs dohrmeer pohr ehl rweedoh*
Could you turn the radio down, please?	¿Podría bajar el volumen de la radio? *pohdreeah bahhahr ehl vohloomehn deh lah rahdyoh?*
We're out of toilet paper	Se acabó el papel higiénico. *seh ahkahboh ehl pahpehl eehyehneekoh*
There aren't any.../there's not enough...	No hay.../no hay suficientes... *noh ay.../noh ay soofeesyehntehs...*
The bed linen's dirty	La ropa de cama está sucia *lah rohpah deh kahmah ehstah soosyah*
The room hasn't been cleaned	No han limpiado la habitación *noh ahn leempyahdoh lah ahbeetahsyohn*
The kitchen is not clean	La cocina no está limpia *lah kohseenah noh ehstah leempyah*
The kitchen utensils are dirty	Los utensilios de cocina están sucios *lohs ootehnseelyohs deh kohseenah ehstahn soosyohs*
The heater's not working	La calefacción no funciona *lah kahlehfahksyohn noh foonsyohnah*
There's no (hot) water/electricity	No hay agua (caliente)/electricidad *noh ay ahgwah(kahlyehnteh)/ehlehktreeseedahdh*
...is broken	...está estropeado *...ehstah ehstrohpehahdoh*
Could you have that seen to?	¿Podrían verlo? *pohdreeahn behrloh?*
Could I have another room/site?	¿Tendría otra habitación/sitio para la tienda? *tehndreeah ohtrah ahbeetahsyohn/seetyoh pahrah lah tyehndah?*
The bed creaks terribly	La cama hace mucho ruido *lah kahmah ahseh moochoh rweedoh*
The bed sags	La cama es demasiado blanda *lah kahmah ehs dehmahsyahdoh blahndah*
There are bugs/insects in our room	Hay muchos bichos/insectos en nuestra habitación *ay moochohs beechohs/eensehktohs ehn nooehstrah ahbeetahsyohn*

This place is full of mosquitos | Está lleno de mosquitos
ehstah lyehnoh deh mohskeetohs

– cockroaches | Está lleno de cucarachas
ehstah lyehnoh deh kookahrahchahs

– Brits | Está lleno de ingleses
ehstah lyehnoh deh eenglehsehs

7.5 Departure

See also 8.2 Settling the bill

I'm leaving tomorrow. Could I settle my bill, please? | Mañana me voy. ¿Podría pagar la cuenta ahora?
mahnyahnah meh boy. pohdreeah pahgahr lah kwehntah ahohrah?

What time should we vacate? | ¿A qué hora tenemos que dejar...?
ah keh ohrah tehnehmohs keh dehhahr...?

Could I have my deposit/passport back, please? | ¿Me devuelve la fianza/el pasaporte?
meh dehbwehlbeh lah fyahnsah/ehl pahsahpohrteh?

We're in a terrible hurry | Estamos muy apurados
ehstahmohs mwee ahpoorahdohs

Could you forward my mail to this address? | ¿Podría enviarme la correspondencia a esta dirección?
pohdreeah ehnbyahrmeh lah kohrrehspohndehnsyah ah ehstah deerehksyohn?

Could we leave our luggage here until we leave? | ¿Podríamos dejar el equipaje aquí hasta que nos marchemos?
pohdreeahmohs dehhahr ehl ehkeepahheh ahkee ahstah keh nohs mahrchehmohs?

Thanks for your hospitality | Muchas gracias por la hospitalidad
moochahs grahsyahs pohr lah ohspeetahleedahdh

Money matters

8

8 Money matters

● Bank opening hours vary in Latin American countries. In large cities exchange bureaux and ATMs for the major credit and debit cards can also be found. To exchange currency a passport is required. It is most advisable to take American dollars when travelling to Latin America, instead of any other foreign currency, since they may even be accepted as a local currency in some countries.

Country	Currency
Argentina	peso
Bolivia	boliviano
Chile	peso
Colombia	peso
Costa Rica	colón
Cuba	peso
Dominican Republic	peso
Ecuador	sucre
El Salvador	colón
Guatemala	quetzal
Honduras	lempira
Mexico	peso
Nicaragua	oro
Panama	balboa
Paraguay	guaraní
Peru	sol
Uruguay	peso

8.1 Banks

Where can I find a bank/an exchange office around here?
¿Dónde hay un banco/una oficina de cambios por aquí?
dohndeh ay oon bahnkoh/oonah ohfeeseenah deh kahmbyohs pohr ahkee?

Where can I cash this traveller's cheque/giro cheque?
¿Dónde puedo cambiar este cheque de viajero/este cheque postal?
dohndeh pwehdoh kahmbyahr ehsteh chehkeh deh byahhehroh/ehsteh chehkeh pohstahl?

Can I cash this...here?
¿Puedo cambiar aquí este...?
pwehdoh kahmbyahr ahkee ehsteh...?

Can I withdraw money on my credit card here?
¿Se puede sacar dinero con una tarjeta de crédito?
seh pwehdeh sahkahr deenehroh kohn oonah tahrhehtah deh krehdeetoh?

What's the minimum/maximum amount?
¿Cuál es el mínimo/el máximo?
kwahl ehs ehl meeneemoh/ehl mahxeemoh?

Can I take out less than that?
¿También puedo sacar menos?
tahmbyehn pwehdoh sahkahr mehnohs?

I've had some money transferred here. Has it arrived yet?
He pedido un giro telegráfico. ¿Me ha llegado ya?
eh pehdeedoh oon heeroh tehlehgrahfeekoh. meh ah lyehgahdoh yah?

These are the details of my bank in the UK — Estos son los datos de mi banco en el Reino Unido
ehstohs sohn lohs dahtohs deh mee bahnkoh ehn ehl reynoh ooneedoh

This is my bank/giro number — Este es mi número de cuenta bancaria/de la caja postal
ehsteh ehs mee noomehroh deh kwehntah bahnkahryah/deh lah kahhah pohstahl

I'd like to change some money — Quisiera cambiar dinero
keesyehrah kahmbyahr deenehroh

– pounds into... — Libras esterlinas por...
leebrahs ehstehrleenahs pohr...

– dollars into... — Dólares estadounidenses por...
dohlahrehs ehstahdohooneedehnsehs pohr...

What's the exchange rate? — ¿A cuánto está el cambio?
ah kwahntoh ehstah ehl kahmbyoh?

Could you give me some small change with it? — ¿Me podría dar sencillo/cambio?
meh pohdreeah dahr sehnseelyoh/kahmbyoh?

This is not right — Esto está mal
ehstoh ehstah mahl

Firme aquí — Sign here, please
Tiene que rellenar esto — Fill this out, please
¿Me permite su pasaporte? — Could I see your passport, please?
¿Me permite su carnet de identidad? — Could I see some identification, please?
¿Me permite su tarjeta de la caja postal? — Could I see your girobank card, please?
¿Me permite su tarjeta del banco? — Could I see your bank card, please?

8.2 Settling the bill

Could you put it on my bill? — ¿Podría cargarlo a mi cuenta?
pohdreeah kahrgahrloh ah mee kwehntah?

Does this amount include service? — ¿Está incluido el servicio en esta cifra?
ehstah eenklooeedoh ehl sehrbeesyoh ehn ehstah seefrah?

Can I pay by...? — ¿Puedo pagar con...?
pwehdoh pahgahr kohn...?

Can I pay by credit card? — ¿Puedo pagar con tarjeta de crédito?
pwehdoh pahgahr kohn tahrhehtah deh krehdeetoh?

Can I pay by traveller's cheque? — ¿Puedo pagar con un cheque de viajero?
pwehdoh pahgahr kohn oon chehkeh de byahhehroh?

Can I pay with foreign currency? — ¿Puedo pagar con moneda extranjera?
pwehdoh pahgahr kohn mohnehdah ehxtrahnhehrah?

You've given me too much/you haven't given me enough change — Me ha devuelto de más/de menos
meh ah dehbwehltoh deh mahs/deh mehnohs

Could you check the bill again, please? — ¿Puede volver a hacer la cuenta?
pwehdeh bohlbehr ah ahsehr lah kwehntah?

Could I have a receipt, please? — ¿Podría darme un recibo?
pohdreeah dahrmeh oon rehseeboh?

I don't have enough money on me — No me alcanza el dinero
noh meh ahlkahnsah ehl deenehroh

This is for you — Tenga, esto es para usted
tehngah, ehstoh ehs pahrah oostehdh

Keep the change — Quédese con el vuelto
kehdehseh kohn ehl bwehltoh

No aceptamos tarjetas de crédito/cheques de viajero/moneda extranjera — We don't accept credit cards/traveller's cheques/foreign currency

Post and telephone

9

9 Post and telephone

9.1 Post

For giros, see 8 Money matters

● **Post offices** are open from Monday to Saturday although opening hours vary from country to country. However, some hotels also provide stamps (*estampillas, timbres*). It is advisable to post letters at a post office, rather than in the mail boxes (*buzón*).

giros postales money orders	telegramas telegrams	sellos stamps
paquetes parcels		

Where's...? ¿Dónde está...?
dohndeh ehstah...?

Where's the post office? ¿Dónde hay una oficina de correos por aquí?
dohndeh ay oonah ohfeeseenah deh kohrrehohs pohr ahkee?

Where's the main post office? ¿Dónde está la oficina central de correos?
dohndeh ehstah lah ohfeeseenah sehntrahl deh kohrrehohs?

Where's the postbox? ¿Dónde hay un buzón por aquí?
dohndeh ay oon boosohn pohr ahkee?

Which counter should I go to...? ¿Cuál es la ventanilla para...?
kwahl ehs lah behntahneelyah pahrah...?

– to send a fax ¿Cuál es la ventanilla para enviar un fax?
kwahl ehs lah behntahneelyah pahrah ehnbyahr oon fahx?

– to change money ¿Cuál es la ventanilla para cambiar dinero?
kwahl ehs lah behntahneelyah pahrah kahmbyahr deenehroh?

– to change giro cheques ¿Cuál es la ventanilla para los cheques postales?
kwahl ehs lah behntahneelyah pahrah lohs chehkehs pohstahlehs?

– for a Telegraph Money Order? ¿Cuál es la ventanilla para los giros telegráficos?
kwahl ehs lah behntahneelyah pahrah lohs heerohs tehlehgrahfeekohs?

Poste restante Lista de correos
leestah deh kohrrehohs

Is there any mail for me? My name's... ¿Hay carta para mí? Me llamo...
ay kahrtah pahrah mee? meh lyahmoh...

Stamps

What's the postage for a...to...? — ¿Cuánto se le pone a un(a)...para...?
kwahntoh seh leh pohneh ah oon(ah)...pahrah...?

Are there enough stamps on it? — ¿Lleva suficiente franqueo?
lyehbah soofeesyehnteh frahnkehoh?

I'd like... ... stamps — Déme... estampillas/timbres de...
dehmeh... ehstahmpeelyahs/teembrehs deh...

I'd like to send this... — Quisiera enviar esto...
keesyehrah ehnbyahr ehstoh...

– express — Quisiera enviar esto por correo urgente
keesyehrah ehnbyahr ehstoh pohr kohrrehoh oorhehnteh

– by air mail — Quisiera enviar esto por avión
keesyehrah ehnbyahr ehstoh pohr ahbyohn

– by registered mail — Quisiera enviar esto certificado
keesyehrah ehnbyahr ehstoh sehrteefeekahdoh

Telegram / fax

I'd like to send a telegram to... — Quisiera mandar un telegrama a...
keesyehrah mahndahr oon tehlehgrahmah ah...

How much is that per word? — ¿Cuánto cuesta por palabra?
kwahntoh kwehstah pohr pahlahbrah?

This is the text I want to send — Este es el texto que quiero enviar
ehsteh ehs ehl tehxtoh keh kyehroh ehnbyahr

Shall I fill in the form myself? — ¿Relleno yo mismo el formulario?
rehlyehnoh yoh meesmoh ehl fohrmoolahryoh?

Can I make photocopies/send a fax here? — ¿Se pueden hacer fotocopias/se puede enviar un fax aquí?
seh pwehdehn ahsehr fohtohkohpyahs/seh pwehdeh ehnbyahr oon fahx ahkee?

How much is it per page? — ¿Cuánto cuesta por página?
kwahntoh kwehstah pohr pahheenah?

9.2 Telephone

See also 1.8 Telephone alphabet

● **For international calls** you may have to go to a telephone office in some Latin American countries, since telephone boxes normally offer access to the local or the interurban network only. The country code for the UK is 44 and 1 for the USA and Canada.

Is there a phone box around here? — ¿Hay alguna caseta/cabina teléfonica por aquí?
ay ahlgoonah kahsehtah/kahbeenah tehlehfohneekah pohr ahkee?

Could I use your phone, please? — ¿Podría usar su teléfono?
pohdreeah oosahr soo tehlehfohnoh?

Do you have a (city/region)...phone directory?	**¿Tiene una guía de teléfonos de la ciudad/la provincia de...?** *tyehneh oonah gheeah deh tehlehfohnohs deh lah syoodahdh/lah prohbeensyah deh...?*
Where can I get a phone card?	**¿Dónde puedo conseguir una tarjeta de teléfonos?** *dohndeh pwehdoh kohnsehgheer oonah tahrhehtah deh tehlehfohnohs?*
Could you give me...?	**¿Me podría dar...?** *meh pohdreeah dahr...?*
– the number for international directory enquiries	**¿Me podría dar el número de información internacional?** *meh pohdreeah dahr ehl noomehroh deh eenfohrmahsyohn eentehrnahsyohnahl?*
– the number of room...	**¿Me podría dar el número de la habitación...?** *meh pohdreeah dahr ehl noomehroh deh lah ahbeetahsyohn...?*
– the international access code	**¿Me podría dar el código internacional?** *meh pohdreeah dahr ehl kohdeegoh eentehrnahsyonahl...?*
– the country code for...	**¿Me podría dar el código de...?** *meh pohdreeah dahr ehl kohdeegoh deh...?*
– the trunk code for...	**¿Me podría dar el prefijo de...?** *meh pohdreeah dahr ehl prehfeehoh deh...?*
– the number of...	**¿Me podría dar el número de...?** *meh pohdreeah dahr ehl noomehroh deh...?*
Could you check if this number's correct?	**¿Podría controlar/revisar si está bien este número?** *pohdreeah kohntrohlahr/rehbeesar see ehstah byehn ehsteh noomehroh?*
Can I dial international direct?	**¿Se puede llamar directamente al extranjero?** *seh pwehdeh lyahmahr deerehktahmehnteh ahl ehxtrahnhehroh?*
Do I have to go through the switchboard?	**¿Hay que llamar por operadora?** *ay keh lyahmahr pohr ohpehrahdohrah?*
Do I have to dial '0' first?	**¿Hay que marcar primero el cero?** *ay keh mahrkahr preemehroh ehl sehroh?*
Do I have to book my calls?	**¿Hay que pedir línea?** *ay keh pehdeer leenehah?*
Could you dial this number for me, please?	**¿Podría usted llamar a este número?** *pohdreeah oostehdh lyahmahr ah ehsteh noomehroh?*
Could you put me through to.../extension..., please?	**¿Me podría poner con.../con la extensión...?** *meh pohdreeah pohnehr kohn.../kohn lah ehxtehnsyohn...?*
I'd like to place a reverse-charge call to...	**Quisiera una llamada de cobro revertido/por cobrar a...** *keesyehrah oonah lyahmahdah deh kohbroh rehbehrteedoh/pohr kohbrahr ah...*
What's the charge per minute?	**¿Cuánto cuesta por minuto?** *kwahntoh kwehstah pohr meenootoh?*
Have there been any calls for me?	**¿Ha habido alguna llamada para mí?** *ah ahbeedoh ahlgoonah lyahmahdah pahrah mee?*

The conversation

Hello, this is...	Buenos días, soy...	*bwehnohs deeahs, soy...*
Who is this, please?	¿Con quién hablo?	*kohn kyehn ahbloh?*
Is this...?	¿Hablo con...?	*ahbloh kohn...?*
I'm sorry, I've dialled the wrong number	Perdone, me he equivocado de número	*pehrdohneh, meh eh ehkeebohkahdoh deh noomehroh*
I can't hear you	No le oigo bien	*noh leh oygoh byehn*
I'd like to speak to...	Quisiera hablar con...	*keesyehrah ahblahr kohn...*
Is there anybody who speaks English?	¿Hay alguien que hable inglés?	*ay ahlghyehn keh ahbleh eenglehs?*
Extension..., please	¿Me pone con la extensión...?	*meh pohneh kohn lah ehxtehnsyohn...?*
Could you ask him/her to call me back?	¿Podría decirle que me llame?	*pohdreeah dehseerleh keh meh lyahmeh?*
My name's... My number's...	Me llamo...Mi número es...	*meh lyahmoh...mee noomehroh ehs...*
Could you tell him/her I called?	¿Puede decirle que llamé?	*pwehdeh dehseerleh keh lyahmeh?*
I'll call back tomorrow	Lo/la volveré a llamar mañana	*loh/lah bohlbehreh ah lyahmahr mahnyahnah*

Lo llaman por teléfono	There's a phone call for you
Primero tiene que marcar el cero	You have to dial '0' first
Un momento, por favor	One moment, please
No contestan	There's no answer
Está ocupado	The line's engaged
¿Quiere esperar?	Do you want to hold?
Ahora le paso	Putting you through
Se ha equivocado de número	You've got a wrong number
El señor/la señora...no está en estos momentos.	He's/she's not here right now
El señor/la señora...no estará hasta...	He'll/she'll be back...
Este es el contestador automático de...	This is the answering machine of...

Shopping

10 Shopping

● **Opening times** for shopping vary in Latin American countries. In large cities, shops and offices remain open at lunch time, but in provinces they may close for long breaks, until late in the afternoon (*siesta*).
Chemists may display the list of *farmacias de guardia* (those open on Sundays and after hours).

almacén
department store
antigüedades
antiques
artículos de deporte
sports shop
artículos del hogar
household goods
artículos dietéticos
health food shop
artículos fotográficos
camera shop
articulos de limpieza
household products and cosmetics
artículos usados
second hand goods
autoservicio
self service
bicicletas
bicycle shop
bodega
off licence
bricolaje
DIY-store
carnicería
butcher's shop
casa de música
music shop
centro comercial
shopping centre
comestibles
grocery store

decoración (de interiores)
interior design shop
droguería
drugstore
electrodomésticos
electrical appliances
farmacia
chemist
ferretería
hardware shop
floristería/florería
florist
frutas y verduras
greengrocer
galería comercial
shopping arcade
heladería
ice cream parlour
joyería
jeweller
juguetería
toy shop
lavandería
laundry
lechería
dairy
librería
book shop
mercado
market
mercería
draper
óptica
optician

panadería
bakery
pastelería/confitería
cake shop
peluquería (señoras, caballeros)
hairdresser
perfumería
cosmetics
pescadería
fishmonger
quiosco
news stand
recuerdos de viaje
souvenir shop
reparación de bicicletas
bicycle repair shop
revistas y prensa
newsagent
salón de belleza
beauty parlour
supermercado
supermarket
tienda/negocio
shop
tienda de modas
clothes shop
tintorería
drycleaner
zapatería
shoe shop
zapatero
cobbler

10.1 Shopping conversations

Where can I get...? — ¿Dónde puedo conseguir...?
dohndeh pwehdoh kohnsehgheer...?

When does this shop open? — ¿De qué hora a qué hora abren?
deh keh ohrah ah keh ohrah ahbrehn?

Could you tell me where the...department is? — ¿Me podría indicar la sección de...?
meh pohdreeah eendeekahr lah sehksyohn deh...?

Could you help me, please? I'm looking for... — ¿Podría ayudarme? Busco...
pohdreeah ahyoodahrmeh? booskoh...

Do you sell British/American newspapers? — ¿Venden periódicos/diarios británicos/americanos?
behndehn pehryohdeekohs/dyahryohs breetahneekohs/ahmehreekahnohs?

¿Lo/la atienden? — Are you being served?

No. I'd like... — No. Quisiera...
noh. keesyehrah...

I'm just looking, if that's all right — Sólo estoy mirando, gracias
sohloh ehstoy meerahndoh, grahsyahs

¿Algo más? — Anything else?

Yes, I'd also like... — Sí, también déme...
see, tahmbyehn dehmeh...

No, thank you. That's all — No, gracias. Es todo
noh, grahsyahs, ehs tohdoh

Could you show me...? — ¿Me podría mostrar...?
meh pohdreeah mohstrahr...?

I'd prefer... — Prefiero...
prehfyehroh...

This is not what I'm looking for — No es lo que busco
noh ehs loh keh booskoh

Thank you. I'll keep looking — Gracias. Voy a seguir mirando
grahsyahs. boy ah sehgheer meerahndoh

Do you have something...? — ¿No tendría algo ...?
noh tehndreeah ahlgoh ...?

– less expensive? — ¿No tendría algo más barato?
noh tehndreeah ahlgoh mahs bahrahtoh?

– smaller? — ¿No tendría algo más pequeño?
noh tehndreeah ahlgoh mahs pehkehnyoh?

– larger? — ¿No tendría algo más grande?
noh tehndreeah ahlgoh mahs grahndeh?

I'll take this one — Me llevo éste/ésta
meh lyehboh ehsteh/ehstah

Does it come with instructions? — ¿Viene con instrucciones?
byehneh kohn eenstrooksyohnehs?

It's too expensive — Me parece muy caro
meh pahrehseh mwee kahroh

I'll give you...	Le doy... *leh doy...*
Could you keep this for me? I'll come back for it later	¿Me lo/la podría guardar? Volveré más tarde a buscarlo *meh loh/lah pohdreeah gwahrdahr? bohlbehreh mahs tahrdeh ah booskahrloh*
Have you got a bag for me, please?	¿Tendría una bolsita? *tehndreeah oonah bohlseetah?*
Could you giftwrap it, please?	¿Me lo podría envolver para regalo? *meh loh pohdreeah ehnbohlbehr pahrah rehgahloh?*

Lo siento; no lo tenemos	I'm sorry, we don't have that
Lo siento; ya no queda	I'm sorry, we're sold out
Lo siento, hasta el...no lo tendremos	I'm sorry, that won't be in until...
Pague en la caja, por favor	You can pay at the cash desk
No aceptamos tarjetas de crédito	We don't accept credit cards
No aceptamos cheques de viajero	We don't accept traveller's cheques
No aceptamos moneda extranjera	We don't accept foreign currency

10.2 Food

I'd like a hundred grams of..., please	Quisiera cien gramos de... *keesyehrah syehn grahmohs deh...*
– half a kilo of...	Quisiera medio kilo de... *keesyehrah mehdyoh keeloh deh...*
– a kilo of...	Quisiera un kilo de... *keesyehrah oon keeloh deh...*
Could you...it for me, please?	¿Me lo podría...? *meh loh pohdreeah...?*
Could you slice it/dice it for me, please?	¿Me lo podría cortar en tajadas/lonchas/rebanadas/trozos? *meh loh pohdreeah kohrtahr ehn tahhahdahs/lohnchahs/rehbahnahdas/trohsohs?*
Could you grate it for me, please?	¿Me lo podría rallar? *meh loh pohdreeah rahlyahr?*
Can I order it?	¿Se lo podría encargar? *seh loh pohdreeah ehnkahrgahr?*
I'll pick it up tomorrow/at...	Pasaré a buscarlo mañana/a las... *pahsahreh ah booskahrloh mahnyahnah/ah lahs...*
Can you eat/drink this?	¿Es para comer/beber? *ehs pahrah kohmehr/behbehr?*
What's in it?	¿Qué lleva dentro? *keh lyehbah dehntroh?*

10.3 Clothing and shoes

I saw something in the window. Shall I point it out?	Vi algo en el escaparate/la vidriera. ¿Se lo enseño? *bee ahlgoh ehn ehl ehskahpahrahteh/ lah beedryehrah, seh loh ehnsehnyoh?*
I'd like something to go with this	Busco algo que haga juego con esto *booskoh ahlgoh keh ahgah hwehgoh kohn ehstoh*
Do you have shoes in this colour?	¿Tiene zapatos de este color? *tyehneh sahpahtohs deh ehsteh kohlohr?*
I'm a size...in the UK	En el Reino Unido tengo el número... *ehn ehl reheenoh ooneedoh tehngoh ehl noomehroh...*
Can I try this on?	¿Me lo podría probar? *meh loh pohdreeah prohbahr?*
Where's the fitting room?	¿Dónde está el probador? *dohndeh ehstah ehl prohbahdohr?*
It doesn't fit	No me queda bien *noh meh kehdah byehn*
This is the right size	Este es mi número *ehsteh ehs mee noomehroh*
It doesn't suit me	No me está bien *noh meh ehstah byehn*
Do you have this/ these in...?	¿Tiene éste/ésta, pero en...? *tyehneh ehsteh/ehstah pehroh ehn...?*
The heel's too high/low	El tacó/tacón me parece muy alto/bajo *ehl tahkoh/tahkohn meh pahrehtheh mwee ahltoh/bahhoh*
Is this/are these genuine leather?	¿Es/son de piel/cuero auténtico/a? *ehs/sohn deh pyehl/kwehroh ah-ootehnteekoh/ah?*
I'm looking for a... for a...-year-old baby/child	Busco un/una...para un bebé/niño de...años *booskoh oon/oonah...pahrah oon behbeh/neenyoh deh...ahnyohs*
I'd like a... ...	Quisiera un/una...de... *keesyehrah oon/oonah...deh...*
– silk	Quisiera un/una...de seda *keesyehrah oon/oonah...deh sehdah*
– cotton	Quisiera un/una...de algodón *keesyehrah oon/oonah...deh ahlgohdohn*
– woollen	Quisiera un/una...de lana *keesyehrah oon/oonah...deh lahnah*
– linen	Quisiera un/una...de hilo/lino *keesyehrah oon/oonah...deh eeloh/leenoh*
What temperature can I wash it at?	¿A qué temperatura lo puedo lavar? *ah keh tehmpehrahtoorah loh pwehdoh lahbahr?*
Will it shrink in the wash?	¿Encoge al lavarlo? *enkohheh ahl lahbahrloh?*

No planchar Do not iron	Colgar mojado Drip dry	Lavado a mano Hand wash
No centrifugar Do not spin dry	Lavado en seco Dry clean	Lavado a máquina Machine wash

At the cobbler

Could you mend these shoes?	¿Podría arreglar estos zapatos? *pohdreeah ahrrehglahr ehstohs sahpahtohs?*
Could you put new soles/heels on these?	¿Podría ponerle suelas nuevas/tacones nuevos? *pohdreeah pohnehrleh swehlahs nwehbahs/ tahkohnehs nwehbohs?*
When will they be ready?	¿Para cuándo van a estar? *pahrah kwahndoh bahn ah ehstahr?*
I'd like..., please	Quisiera..., por favor *keesyehrah..., pohr fahbohr*
– a tin of shoe polish	Quisiera una crema para zapatos *keesyehrah oonah krehmah pahrah sahpahtohs*
– a pair of shoelaces	Quisiera un par de cordones *keesyehrah oon pahr deh kohrdohnehs*

10.4 Photographs and video

I'd like a film for this camera, please	Quisiera un rollo/carrete para esta cámara *keesyehrah oon rohlyoh/kahrrehteh pahrah ehstah kahmahrah*
– a 126 cartridge	Quisiera una película en cassette de 126 *keesyehrah oonah pehleekoolah ehn kahseht deh syehntoh beheenteesehees*
– a 35mm colour slide	Quisiera un rollo/carrete de 35mm para diapositivas en color *keesyehrah oon rohlyoh/kahrrehteh deh treyntah ee seenkoh meeleemehtrohs pahrah deeapohseeteebahs ehn kohlohr*
– a 35mm colour print	Quisiera un rollo/carrete de 35mm en color *keesyehrah oon rohlyoh/kahrrehteh deh treyntah ee seenkoh meeleemehtrohs ehn kohlohr*
– a 35mm black and white	Quisiera un rollo/carrete de 35mm en blanco y negro *keesyehrah oon rohlyoh/kahrrehteh deh treyntah ee seenkoh meeleemehtrohs ehn blahnkoh ee nehgroh*
– a videotape	Quisiera una cinta de vídeo *keesyehrah oonah seentah deh veedehoh*
colour/black and white	color/blanco y negro *kohlohr/blahnkoh ee nehgroh*
super eight	superocho *soopehrohchoh*
12/24/36 exposures	doce/veinticuatro/treinta y seis fotos *dohseh/beheenteekwahtroh/treheentah ee sehees fohtohs*
ASA/DIN number	valor ISO *bahlohr eesoh*
daylight film	película para luz natural *pehleekoolah pahrah loos nahtoorahl*
film for artificial light	película para luz artificial *pehleekoolah pahrah loos ahrteefeesyahl*

Problems

Could you load the film for me, please?	¿Me podría poner el rollo/carrete en la cámara?	*meh pohdreeah pohnehr ehl rohlyoh/kahrrehteh ehn lah kahmahrah?*
Could you take the film out for me, please?	¿Me podría sacar el rollo/carrete de la cámara?	*meh pohdreeah sahkahr ehl rohlyoh/kahrrehteh deh lah kahmahrah?*
Should I replace the batteries?	¿Tengo que cambiar las pilas?	*tehngoh keh kahmbyahr lahs peelahs?*
Could you have a look at my camera, please? It's not working	¿Me podría revisar la cámara? Ya no funciona	*meh pohdreeah rehbeesahr lah kahmahrah? yah noh foonsyohnah*
The...is broken	Está estropeado el...	*ehstah ehstrohpehahdoh ehl...*
The film's jammed	Se ha atascado el rollo/carrete	*seh ah ahtahskahdoh ehl rohlyoh /kahrrehteh*
The film's broken	Se ha roto el rollo/carrete	*seh ah rohtoh ehl rohlyoh/kahrrehteh*
The flash isn't working	No funciona el flash	*noh foonsyohnah ehl flahsh*

Processing and prints

I'd like to have this film developed/printed, please	Quisiera mandar a revelar/copiar este rollo/carrete	*keesyehrah mahndahr ah rehbehlahr/kohpyahr ehsteh rohlyoh/kahrrehteh*
I'd like...prints from each negative	Quisiera...copias de cada negativo	*keesyehrah...kohpyahs deh kahdah nehgahteeboh*
glossy/mat	brillante/mate	*breelyahnte/mahteh*
I'd like to reorder these photos	Quisiera encargar más copias de estas fotos	*keesyehrah ehnkahrgahr mahs kohpyahs deh ehstahs fohtohs*
I'd like to have this photo enlarged	Quisiera una ampliación de esta foto	*keesyehrah oonah ahmplyahsyohn deh ehstah fohtoh*
How much is processing?	¿Cuánto sale el revelado?	*kwahntoh sahleh ehl rehbehlahdoh?*
– printing?	¿Cuánto sale el copiado?	*kwahntoh sahleh ehl kohpyahdoh?*
– extra copies?	¿Cuánto salen las copias adicionales?	*kwahntoh sahlehn lahs kohpyahs ahdeesyohnahlehs?*
– the enlargement?	¿Cuánto sale la ampliación?	*kwahntoh sahleh lah ahmplyahsyohn?*
When will they be ready?	¿Para cuándo van a estar?	*pahrah kwahndoh bahn ah ehstahr?*

10.5 At the hairdresser's

Do I have to make an appointment?	¿Tengo que pedir hora/cita? *tehngoh keh pehdeer ohrah/seetah?*
Can I come in straight away?	¿Podría atenderme enseguida? *pohdreeah ahtehndehrmeh ehnsehgheedah?*
How long will I have to wait?	¿Cuánto tengo que esperar? *kwahntoh tehngoh keh ehspehrahr?*
I'd like a shampoo/ haircut	Quisiera lavarme/cortarme el pelo *keesyehrah lahbahrmeh/kohrtahrmeh ehl pehloh*
I'd like a shampoo for oily/dry hair, please	Quisiera un champú para cabello graso/seco *keesyehrah oon chahmpoo pahrah kahbehlyoh grahsoh/sehkoh*
– an anti-dandruff shampoo	Quisiera un champú anticaspa *keesyehrah oon chahmpoo ahnteekahspah*
– a shampoo for permed/coloured hair	Quisiera un champú para cabello con permanente/teñido. *keesyehrah oon chahmpoo pahrah kahbehlyoh kohn pehrmahnehnteh/tehnyeedoh*
– a colour rinse shampoo	Quisiera un champú color *keesyehrah oon chahmpoo kohlohr*
– a shampoo with conditioner	Quisiera un champú con acondicionador *keesyehrah oon chahmpoo kohn ahkohndeesyohnahdohr*
– highlights	Quisiera que me hagan claritos/luces *keesyehrah keh meh ahgahn klahreetohs/ loosehs*
Do you have a colour chart, please?	¿Tendría una carta de colores? *tehndreeah oonah kahrtah deh kohlohrehs?*
I want to keep it the same colour	Quiero conservar el mismo color *kyehroh kohnsehrbahr ehl meesmoh kohlohr*
I'd like it darker/lighter	Quisiera un color más oscuro/más claro *keesyehrah oon kohlohr mahs ohskooroh/mahs klahroh*
I'd like/I don't want hairspray	(No) quiero fijador *(noh) kyehroh feehahdohr*
– gel	(No) quiero gel *(noh) kyehroh hehl*
– lotion	(No) quiero loción *(noh) kyehroh lohsyohn*
I'd like a short fringe	Quisiera el flequillo corto *keesyehrah ehl flehkeelyoh kohrtoh*
Not too short at the back	No lo quisiera demasiado corto por detrás *noh loh keesyehrah dehmahsyahdoh kohrtoh pohr dehtrahs*
Not too long here	No lo quisiera demasiado largo aquí *noh loh keesyehrah dehmahsyahdoh lahrgoh ahkee*
I'd like/I don't want (many) curls	(No) quisiera (demasiados) rizos *(noh) keesyehrah (dehmahsyadohs) reesohs*

It needs a little/ a lot taken off	Hay que cortar sólo un trocito/un buen trozo	*ay keh kohrtahr sohloh oon trohseetoh/oon bwehn trohsoh*
I want a completely different style	Quisiera un modelo totalmente diferente	*keesyehrah oon mohdehloh tohtahlmehnteh deefehrehnteh*
I'd like it the same as...	Quisiera el pelo como...	*keesyehrah ehl pehloh kohmoh...*
– as that lady's	Quisiera el pelo como esa señora	*keesyehrah ehl pehloh kohmoh ehsah sehnyohrah*
– as in this photo	Quisiera el pelo como en esta foto	*keesyehrah ehl pehloh kohmoh ehn ehstah fohtoh*
Could you put the drier up/down a bit?	¿Podría poner el casco más alto/bajo?	*pohdreeah pohnehr ehl kahskoh mahs ahltoh/mahs bahhoh?*
I'd like a facial	Quisiera una máscara facial	*keesyehrah oonah mahskahrah fahsyahl*
– a manicure	Quisiera que me hagan manicura	*keesyehrah keh meh ahgahn mahneekoorah*
– a massage	Quisiera que me hagan masaje	*keesyehrah keh meh ahgahn mahsahheh*
Could you trim my fringe?	¿Me podría recortar el flequillo?	*meh pohdreeah rehkohrtahr ehl flehkeelyoh?*
– my beard?	¿Me podría recortar la barba?	*meh pohdreeah rehkohrtahr lah bahrbah?*
– my moustache?	¿Me podría recortar el bigote?	*meh pohdreeah rehkohrtahr ehl beegohteh?*
I'd like a shave, please	Aféiteme/rasúreme, por favor	*ahfeheetehmeh/rahsoorehmeh, pohr fahbohr*
I'd like a wet shave, please	Aféiteme/rasúreme a navaja, por favor	*ahfeheetehmeh/rahsoorehmeh ah nahbahhah, pohr fahbohr*

¿Cómo quiere el corte de pelo?	How do you want it cut?
¿Qué modelo deseaba?	What style did you have in mind?
¿Qué color quiere?	What colour do you want it?
¿Esta temperatura le va bien?	Is the temperature all right for you?
¿Quiere algo para leer?	Would you like something to read?
¿Quiere algo para beber?	Would you like a drink?
¿Así está bien?	Is this what you had in mind?

At the Tourist Information Centre

11

11 At the Tourist Information Centre

11.1 Places of interest

Where's the Tourist Information, please?	¿Dónde está la oficina de turismo? *dohndeh ehstah lah ohfeeseenah deh tooreesmoh?*
Do you have a city map?	¿Tendría un plano de la ciudad? *tehndreeah oon plahnoh deh lah syoodahdh?*
Where is the museum?	¿Dónde está el museo? *dohndeh ehstah ehl moosehoh?*
Where can I find a church?	¿Dónde podría encontrar una iglesia? *dohndeh pohdreeah ehnkohntrahr oonah eeglehsyah?*
Could you give me some information about...?	¿Me podría dar información sobre...? *meh pohdreeah dahr eenfohrmahsyohn sohbreh...?*
How much is that?	¿Cuánto le debemos por esto? *kwahntoh leh dehbehmohs pohr ehstoh?*
What are the main places of interest?	¿Cuáles son los sitios más interesantes para visitar? *kwahlehs sohn lohs seetyohs mahs eentehrehsahntehs pahrah veeseetahr?*
Could you point them out on the map?	¿Me los podría señalar en el plano? *meh lohs pohdreeah sehnyahlahr ehn ehl plahnoh?*
What do you recommend?	¿Qué nos recomienda? *keh nohs rehkohmyehndah?*
We'll be here for a few hours	Pensamos quedarnos unas horas *pehnsahmohs kehdahrnohs oonahs ohrahs*
– a day	Pensamos quedarnos un día *pehnsahmohs kehdahrnohs oon deeah*
– a week	Pensamos quedarnos una semana *pehnsahmohs kehdahrnohs oonah sehmahnah*
We're interested in...	Nos interesa... *nohs eentehrehsah...*
Is there a scenic walk around the city?	¿Hay algún circuito turístico para visitar la ciudad a pie? *ay ahlgoon seerkweetoh tooreesteekoh pahrah veeseetar lah syoodahdh ah pyeh?*
How long does it take?	¿Cuánto dura? *kwahntoh doorah?*
Where does it start/end?	¿De dónde sale?/¿Dónde termina? *deh dohndeh sahleh?/dohndeh tehrmeenah?*
Are there any boat cruises here?	¿Hay excursiones en barco? *ay ehxkoorsyohnehs ehn bahrkoh?*
Where can we board?	¿Dónde se puede embarcar? *dohndeh seh pwehdeh ehmbahrkahr?*
Are there any bus tours?	¿Hay excursiones en autocar? *ay ehxkoorsyohnehs ehn ahootohkahr?*
Where do we get on?	¿De dónde salen? *deh dohndeh sahlehn?*
Is there a guide who speaks English?	¿Hay algún guía que hable inglés? *ay ahlgoon gheeah keh ahbleh eenglehs?*

What trips can we take around the area?	¿Qué excursiones se pueden hacer en los alrededores? *keh ehxkoorsyohnehs seh pwehdehn ahsehr ehn lohs ahlrehdehdohrehs?*
Are there any excursions?	¿Hay excursiones organizadas? *ay ehxkoorsyohnehs ohrgahneesahdahs?*
Where do they go to?	¿Hacia dónde van? *ahsyah dohndeh bahn?*
We'd like to go to...	Quisiéramos ir a... *keesyehrahmohs eer ah...*
How long is the trip?	¿Cuánto se tarda en llegar? *kwahntoh seh tahrdah ehn lyehgahr?*
How long do we stay in...?	¿Cuánto dura la visita a...? *kwahntoh doorah lah beeseetah ah...*
Are there any guided tours?	¿Hay visitas guiadas? *ay beeseetahs gheeahdahs?*
How much free time will we have there?	¿Cuánto tiempo libre tenemos allí? *kwahntoh tyehmpoh leebreh tehnehmohs ahlyee?*
We want to go hiking	Nos gustaría hacer una excursión a pie *nohs goostahreeah ahsehr oonah ehxkoorsyohn ah pyeh*
Can we hire a guide?	¿Es posible contratar un guía? *ehs pohseebleh kohntrahtahr oon gheeah?*
Can I book mountain huts?	¿Se puede hacer una reserva/reservación para un refugio (en la montaña)? *seh pwehdeh ahsehr oonah rehsehrbah/ rehsehrbahsyohn pahrah oon rehfoohyoh (ehn lah mohntahnyah)?*
What time does... open/close?	¿A qué hora abre/cierra...? *ah keh ohrah ahbreh/syehrrah...?*
What days is...open/ closed?	¿Qué días tiene abierto/cerrado...? *keh deeahs tyehneh ahbyehrtoh/sehrrahdoh...?*
What's the admission price?	¿Cuánto sale la entrada? *kwahntoh sahleh lah ehntrahdah?*
Is there a group discount?	¿Hay descuento para grupos? *ay dehskwehntoh pahrah groopohs?*
Is there a child discount?	¿Hay descuento para niños? *ay dehskwehntoh pahrah neenyohs?*
Is there a discount for pensioners?	¿Hay descuento para jubilados? *ay dehskwehntoh pahrah hoobeelahdohs?*
Can I take (flash) photos/can I film here?	¿Se pueden sacar fotos (con flash)/ filmar aquí? *seh pwehdehn sahkahr fohtohs(kohn flahsh)/feelmahr ahkee?*
Do you have any postcards of...?	¿Venden postales de...? *behndehn pohstahlehs deh...?*
Do you have an English...?	¿Tiene un...en inglés? *tyehneh oon...ehn eenglehs?*
– an English catalogue?	¿Tiene un catálogo en inglés? *tyehneh oon kahtahlohgoh ehn eenglehs?*
– an English programme?	¿Tiene un programa en inglés? *tyehneh oon prohgrahmah ehn eenglehs?*
– an English brochure?	¿Tiene un folleto en inglés? *tyehneh oon fohlyehtoh ehn eenglehs?*

11.2 Going out

Do you have this week's/month's entertainment guide?	¿Tiene la guía de los espectáculos de esta semana/este mes? *tyehneh lah gheeah deh lohs ehspehktahkoolohs deh ehstah sehmahnah/ehsteh mehs?*
What's on tonight?	¿Adónde podríamos ir esta noche? *ahdohndeh pohdreeahmohs eer ehstah nohcheh?*
We want to go to...	Nos gustaría ir a... *nohs goostahreeah eer ah...*
Which films are showing?	¿Qué películas dan? *keh pehleekoolahs dahn?*
What sort of film is that?	¿Qué clase de película es? *keh klahseh deh pehleekoolah ehs?*
suitable for everyone	para todos los públicos *pahrah tohdohs lohs poobleekohs*
not suitable for children	prohibido para menores de 12/16 años *proheebeedoh pahrah mehnohrehs deh dohseh/dyehseesehees ahnyohs*
original version	versión original *behrsyohn ohreeheenahl*
subtitled	subtitulada *soobteetoolahdah*
dubbed	doblada *dohblahdah*
Is it a continuous showing?	¿Es sesión continua? *ehs sehsyohn kohnteenooah?*
What's on at...?	¿Qué dan en...? *keh dahn ehn...?*
– the theatre?	¿Qué dan en el teatro? *keh dahn ehn ehl tehahtroh?*
– the concert hall?	¿Qué tocan en la sala de conciertos? *keh tohkahn ehn lah sahlah deh kohnsyehrtohs?*
– the opera?	¿Qué dan en la ópera? *keh dahn ehn lah ohpehrah?*
Where can I find a good disco around here?	¿Dónde hay una buena discoteca por aquí? *dohndeh ay oonah bwehnah deeskohtehkah pohr ahkee?*
Is it for members only?	¿Hay que ser socio? *ay keh sehr sohsyoh?*
Where can I find a good cabaret club around here?	¿Dónde hay un buen cabaret por aquí? *dohndeh ay oon bwehn kahbahreh pohr ahkee?*
Is it evening wear only?	¿Hay que ir en traje de etiqueta? *ay keh eer ehn trahheh deh ehteekehtah?*
Should I/we dress up?	¿Es recomendable ir en traje de etiqueta? *ehs rehkohmehndahbleh eer ehn trahheh deh ehteekehtah?*
What time does the show start?	¿A qué hora empieza el espectáculo? *ah keh ohrah ehmpyehsah ehl ehspehktahkooloh?*
When's the next soccer match?	¿Cuándo es el próximo partido de fútbol? *kwahndoh ehs ehl prohxeemoh pahrteedoh deh footbohl?*

Who's playing?	¿Quiénes juegan?	*kyehnehs hwehgahn?*
I'd like an escort for tonight. Could you arrange that for me?	Quisiera contratar un/una acompañante para esta noche. ¿Podría hacerme una reserva/reservación?	*keesyehrah kohntrahtahr oon/oonah ahkohmpahnyahnteh pahrah ehstah nohcheh. podreeah ahsehrmeh oonah rehsehrbah/rehsehrbahsyohn?*

11.3 Booking tickets

Could you book some tickets for us?	¿Podría hacernos una reserva/reservación?	*pohdreeah ahsehrnohs oonah rehsehrbah/rehsehrbahsyohn?*
We'd like to book... tickets/a table...	Quisiéramos...entradas/una mesa...	*keesyehrahmohs...ehntrahdahs/oonah mehsah...*
– tickets/seats in the stalls	Quisiéramos...entradas en la platea	*keesyehrahmohs...ehntrahdahs ehn lah plahtehah*
– tickets/seats on the balcony	Quisiéramos...entradas en el palco	*keesyehrahmohs...ehntrahdahs ehn ehl pahlkoh*
– box seats	Quisiéramos...entradas en el palco privado	*keesyehrahmohs...ehntrahdahs ehn ehl pahlkoh preebahdoh*
– a table at the front	Quisiéramos una mesa adelante	*keesyehrahmohs oonah mehsah ahdehlahnteh*
– in the middle	Quisiéramos una mesa al centro	*keesyehrahmohs oonah mehsah ahl sehntroh*
– at the back	Quisiéramos una mesa atrás	*keesyehrahmohs oonah mehsah ahtrahs*
Could I book...seats for the...o'clock performance?	¿Podría reservar...entradas para la función de las...?	*pohdreeah rehsehrbahr...ehntrahdahs pahrah lah foonsyohn deh lahs...?*
Are there any seats left for tonight?	¿Quedan entradas para esta noche?	*kehdahn ehntrahdahs pahrah ehstah nohcheh?*
How much is a ticket?	¿Cuánto sale la entrada?	*kwahntoh sahleh lah ehntrahdah?*
When can I pick the tickets up?	¿Cuándo puedo pasar a retirar/recoger las entradas?	*kwahndoh pwehdoh pahsahr ah rehteerahr/rehkohhehr lahs ehntrahdahs?*
I've got a reservation	Tengo una reserva/reservación	*tehngoh oonah rehsehrbah/rehsehrbahsyohn*
My name's...	Me llamo...	*meh lyahmoh...*

¿Para qué función desea reservar?	Which performance do you want to book for?
¿Qué sector prefiere?	Where would you like to sit?
No hay entradas	Everything's sold out
Sólo quedan entradas de pie	It's standing room only
Sólo quedan entradas en el palco	We've only got balcony seats left
Sólo quedan entradas en la galería	We've only got seats left in the gallery
Sólo quedan entradas en la platea	We've only got stalls seats left
Sólo quedan entradas adelante	We've only got seats left at the front
Sólo quedan entradas atrás	We've only got seats left at the back
¿Cuántas entradas quiere?	How many seats would you like?
Tiene que retirar/recoger las entradas antes de las...	You'll have to pick up the tickets before...o'clock
¿Me permite las entradas?	Tickets, please
Este es su asiento	This is your seat

12 Sports

12 Sports

12.1 Sporting questions

Where can we... around here?	¿Dónde se puede... por aquí? *dohndeh seh pwehdeh... pohr ahkee?*
Is there a... around here?	¿Hay algún...por aquí cerca? *ahee ahlgoon...pohr ahkee sehrkah?*
Can I hire a...here?	¿Alquilan...? *ahlkeelahn...?*
Can I take...lessons?	¿Dan clases de...? *dahn klahsehs deh...?*
How much is that per hour/per day/class?	¿Cuánto sale por hora/día/clase? *kwahntoh sahleh pohr ohrah/deeah/klahseh?*
Do I need a permit for that?	¿Se necesita un permiso? *seh nehsehseetah oon pehrmeesoh?*
Where can I get the permit?	¿Dónde se consiguen los permisos? *dohndeh seh kohnseeghehn lohs pehrmeesohs?*

12.2 By the waterfront

Is it a long way to the sea still?	¿Falta mucho para llegar al mar? *fahltah moochoh pahrah lyehgahr ahl mahr?*
Is there a...around here?	¿Hay algún...por aquí? *ay ahlgoon...pohr ahkee?*
– an outdoor/indoor/ public swimming pool	¿Hay alguna piscina por aquí? *ay ahlgoonah peesseenah pohr ahkee?*
– a sandy beach	¿Hay alguna playa con arena por aquí? *ay ahlgoonah plahyah kohn ahrehnah pohr ahkee?*
– a nudist beach	¿Hay alguna playa nudista por aquí? *ay ahlgoonah plahyah noodeestah pohr ahkee?*
– mooring	¿Hay algún atracadero por aquí? *ay ahlgoon ahtrahkahdehroh pohr ahkee?*
Are there any rocks here?	¿Hay rocas? *ay rohkahs?*
When's high/low tide?	¿Cuándo sube/baja la marea? *kwahndoh soobeh/bahhah lah mahrehah?*
What's the water temperature?	¿Qué temperatura tiene el agua? *keh tehmpehrahtoorah tyehneh ehl ahgwah?*
Is it (very) deep here?	¿Es (muy) profundo? *ehs mwee prohfoondoh?*
Can you stand here?	¿Se puede estar de pie? *seh pwehdeh ehstahr de pyeh?*
Is it safe to swim here?	¿Es seguro para nadar? *ehs sehgooroh pahrah nahdahr?*
Are there any currents?	¿Hay corriente? *ay kohrryehnteh?*
Are there any rapids/ waterfalls in this river?	¿Este río tiene rápidos/cascadas? *ehsteh reeoh tyehneh rahpeedohs/kahskahdahs?*
What does that flag/ buoy mean?	¿Qué significa aquella bandera/boya? *keh seegneefeekah ahkehlyah bahndehrah/bohyah?*

Is there a life guard on duty here?	¿Hay algún socorrista/guardavidas/salvavidas?	*ay ahlgoon sohkohrreestah/ gwahrdahbeedahs/ sahlbahbeedahs?*
Are dogs allowed here?	¿Está permitido traer perros?	*ehstah pehrmeeteedoh trahehr pehrrohs?*
Is camping on the beach allowed?	¿Está permitido acampar en la playa?	*ehstah pehrmeeteedoh ahkahmpahr ehn lah plahyah?*
Are we allowed to build a fire here?	¿Está permitido hacer fuego?	*ehstah pehrmeeteedoh ahsehr fwehgoh?*

Peligro
Danger

Aguas de pesca
Fishing water

Prohibido pescar
No fishing

Prohibido hacer surfing
No surfing

Prohibido bañarse
No swimming

Permiso obligatorio
Permits only

12 .3 In the snow

Can I take ski lessons here?	¿Dan clases de esquí?	*dahn klahsehs deh eskee?*
for beginners/advanced	para principiantes/avanzados	*pahrah preenseepyahntehs/ahbahnsahdohs*
How large are the groups?	¿De cuántas personas son los grupos?	*deh kwahntahs pehrsohnahs sohn lohs groopohs?*
What language are the classes in?	¿En qué idioma son las clases?	*ehn keh eedyohmah sohn lahs klahsehs?*
I'd like a lift pass, please	Quisiera un pase para las telesillas	*keesyehrah oon pahseh pahrah lahs tehlehseelyahs*
Must I give you a passport photo?	¿Se necesita foto?	*seh nehsehseetah fohtoh?*
Where can I have a passport photo taken?	¿Dónde puedo sacarme fotos?	*dohndeh pwehdoh sahkahrmeh fohtohs?*
Where are the beginners' slopes?	¿Dónde están las pistas para principiantes?	*dohndeh ehstahn lahs peestahs pahrah preenseepyahntehs?*
Are there any runs for cross-country skiing?	¿Hay pistas de esquí de fondo por aquí?	*ay peestahs deh ehskee deh fohndoh pohr ahkee?*
Have the cross-country runs been marked?	¿Las pistas de esquí de fondo están señalizadas?	*lahs peestahs deh ehskee deh fohndoh ehstahn sehnyahleesahdahs?*
Are the...in operation?	¿Están abiertos los...?	*ehstahn ahbyehrtohs lohs...?*
– the ski lifts	¿Ya funcionan los telesquís?	*yah foonsyohnahn lohs tehlehskees?*
– the chair lifts	¿Ya funcionan las telesillas?	*yah foonsyohnahn lahs tehlehseelyahs?*
Are the slopes usable?	¿Están abiertas las pistas?	*ehstahn ahbyehrtahs lahs peestahs?*

13 Sickness

13

13 Sickness

13.1 Call (fetch) the doctor

Could you call/fetch a doctor quickly, please?	¿Podría llamar/ir a buscar rápido a un médico, por favor? *pohdreeah lyahmahr/eer ah booskahr rahpeedoh ah oon mehdeekoh, pohr fahbohr?*
When does the doctor have a surgery?	¿Cuándo atiende/tiene consulta el médico? *kwahndoh ahtyehndeh/tyehneh kohnsooltah ehl mehdeekoh?*
When can the doctor come?	¿Cuándo puede venir el médico? *kwahndoh pwehdeh behneer ehl mehdeekoh?*
I'd like to make an appointment to see the doctor	¿Podría pedirme hora/cita con el médico? *pohdreeah pehdeermeh ohrah/seetah kohn ehl mehdeekoh?*
I've got an appointment to see the doctor at...	Tengo hora/cita con el médico para las... *tehngoh ohrah/seetah kohn ehl mehdeekoh pahrah lahs...*
Which doctor/chemist has night/weekend duty?	¿Qué médico/farmacia está de guardia esta noche/este fin de semana? *keh mehdeekoh/fahrmahsyah ehstah deh gwahrdyah ehstah nohcheh/ehsteh feen deh sehmahnah?*

13.2 Patient's ailments

I don't feel well	No me siento bien *noh meh syehntoh byehn*
I'm dizzy	Tengo mareos *tehngoh mahrehohs*
– ill	Estoy enfermo *ehstoy ehnfehrmoh*
– sick	Tengo náuseas *tehngoh nahoosehahs*
I've got a cold	Estoy acatarrado *ehstoy ahkahtahrrahdoh*
It hurts here	Me duele aquí *meh dwehleh ahkee*
I've been throwing up	He devuelto *eh dehbwehltoh*
I've got...	Tengo molestias de... *tehngoh mohlehstyahs deh...*
I'm running a temperature of...degrees	Tengo...grados de fiebre *tehngoh...grahdohs deh fyehbreh*
I've been stung by a wasp	Me picó una avispa *meh peekoh oonah ahbeespah*
I've been stung by an insect	Me picó un insecto *meh peekoh oon eensehktoh*
I've been bitten by a dog	Me mordó un perro *meh mohrdoh oon pehrroh*
I've been stung by a jellyfish	Me picó una medusa *meh peekoh oonah mehdoosah*

I've been bitten by a snake	Me mordó una serpiente *meh mohrdoh oonah sehrpyehnteh*
I've been bitten by an animal	Me picó un insecto *meh peekoh oon eensehktoh*
I've cut myself	Me corté *meh kohrteh*
I've burned myself	Me quemé *meh kehmeh*
I've grazed myself	Tengo una rozadura *tehngoh oonah rohsahdoorah*
I've had a fall	Me caí *meh kahee*
I've sprained my ankle	Me torcí el tobillo *meh tohrsee ehl tohbeelyoh*
I've come for the morning-after pill	Vengo a que me dé una píldora del día después *behngoh ah keh meh deh oonah peeldohrah dehl deeah dehspwehs*

13.3 The consultation

¿Qué molestias tiene?	What seems to be the problem?
¿Cuánto hace que tiene estas molestias?	How long have you had these symptoms?
¿Ha tenido estas molestias anteriormente?	Have you had this trouble before?
¿Qué temperatura tiene?	How high is your temperature?
Desnúdese	Get undressed, please
Desvístase de la cintura para arriba	Strip to the waist, please
Allí puede quitarse la ropa	You can undress there
Descúbrase el brazo izquierdo/derecho	Roll up your left/right sleeve, please
Recuéstese aquí	Lie down here, please
¿Le duele esto?	Does this hurt?
Respire hondo	Breathe deeply
Abra la boca	Open your mouth

Patient's medical history

I'm a diabetic	Soy diabético *soy deeahbehteekoh*
I have a heart condition	Soy enfermo cardíaco *soy ehnfehrmoh kahrdeeahkoh*
I have asthma	Soy asmático *soy ahsmahteekoh*
I'm allergic to...	Soy alérgico a... *soy ahlehrheekoh ah...*
I'm...months pregnant	Estoy embarazada de...meses *ehstoy ehmbahrahsadah deh...mehsehs*
I'm on a diet	Sigo una dieta *seegoh oonah dyehtah*

I'm on medication/ the pill	Tomo medicamentos/la píldora *tohmoh mehdeekahmehntohs/lah peeldohrah*
I've had a heart attack once before	Ya tuve un ataque cardíaco *yah toobeh oon ahtahkeh kahrdeeahkoh*
I've had a(n)...operation	Me operaron del/de la... *meh ohpehrahrohn dehl/deh lah...*
I've been ill recently	Estuve enfermo hace poco *ehstoobeh ehnfehrmoh ahseh pohkoh*
I've got an ulcer	Tengo una úlcera *tehngoh oonah oolsehrah*
I've got my period	Tengo la regla *tehngoh lah rehglah*

¿Padece alguna alergia?	Do you have any allergies?
¿Toma medicamentos?	Are you on any medication?
¿Sigue alguna dieta?	Are you on a diet?
¿Está embarazada?	Are you pregnant?
¿Está vacunado/a contra el tétanos?	Have you had a tetanus injection?

No es nada grave	It's nothing serious
Se fracturó el/la...	Your...is broken
Se contusionó el/la...	You've got a/some bruised...
Se desgarró el/la...	You've got (a) torn...
Tiene una inflamación	You've got an inflammation
Tiene apendicitis	You've got appendicitis
Tiene bronquitis	You've got bronchitis
Tiene una enfermedad venérea	You've got a venereal disease
Tiene gripe	You've got the flu
Tuvo un ataque al corazón	You've had a heart attack
Tiene una infección vírica/viral, bacteriana	You've got an infection (viral..., bacterial...)
Tiene una pulmonía	You've got pneumonia
Tiene una úlcera	You've got an ulcer
Se distendó un músculo	You've pulled a muscle
Tiene una infección vaginal	You've got a vaginal infection
Tiene una intoxicación alimenticia	You've got food poisoning

Tiene una insolación	You've got sunstroke
Es alérgico a...	You're allergic to...
Está embarazada	You're pregnant
Quisiera hacerle un análisis de sangre/de orina/de materia fecal	I'd like to have your blood/urine/stools tested
Hay que suturar la herida	It needs stitching
Lo/la voy a derivar a un especialista/a un hospital	I'm referring you to a specialist/sending you to hospital
Tiene que hacerse radiografías	You'll need to have some x-rays taken
Vuelva a tomar asiento en la sala de espera	Could you wait in the waiting room, please?
Hay que operarlo/operarla	You'll need an operation

The diagnosis

Is it contagious?	¿Es contagioso? *ehs kohntahhyohsoh?*
How long do I have to stay...?	¿Hasta cuándo tengo que...? *ahstah kwahndoh tehngoh keh...?*
– in bed	¿Hasta cuándo tengo que guardar cama? *ahstah kwahndoh tehngoh keh gwahrdahr kahmah?*
– in hospital	¿Hasta cuándo tengo que quedarme en el hospital? *ahstah kwahndoh tehngoh keh kehdahrmeh ehn ehl ohspeetahl?*
Do I have to go on a special diet?	¿Tengo que seguir alguna dieta? *tehngoh keh sehgheer ahlgoonah dyehtah?*
Am I allowed to travel?	¿Puedo viajar? *pwehdoh byahhahr?*
Can I make a new appointment?	¿Puedo volver a pedir hora/cita? *pwehdoh bohlbehr ah pehdeer ohrah/seetah?*
When do I have to come back?	¿Cuándo tengo que volver? *kwahndoh tehngoh keh bohlbehr?*
I'll come back tomorrow	Vuelvo mañana *bwehlboh mahnyahnah*

Vuelva mañana/dentro de...días	Come back tomorrow/in...days' time

13.4 Medication and prescriptions

How do I take this medicine?	¿Cómo se toman estos medicamentos? *kohmoh seh tohmahn ehstohs mehdeekahmehntohs?*
How many capsules/drops/injections/spoonfuls/tablets each time?	¿Cuántas cápsulas/gotas/inyecciones/cucharadas/tabletas por vez? *kwahntahs kahpsoolahs/gohtahs/eenyehksyohnehs/koochahrahdahs pohr behs?*

How many times a day? — ¿Cuántas veces al día?
kwahntahs behsehs ahl deeah?

I've forgotten my medication. At home I take... — Se me ha olvidado traer los medicamentos. En casa tomo...
seh meh ah olbeedahdoh trahehr lohs mehdeekahmehntohs. ehn kahsah tohmoh...

Could you make out a prescription for me? — ¿Podría hacerme una receta?
pohdreeah ahsehrmeh oonah rehsehtah?

Voy a recetarle unos antibióticos/un jarabe/un calmante/ unos analgésicos — I'm prescribing antibiotics/a mixture/a tranquillizer/pain killers
Tiene que guardar reposo — Have lots of rest
No tiene que salir a la calle — Stay indoors
Tiene que guardar cama — Stay in bed

---

antes de cada comida
before meals
cápsulas
capsules
diluir en agua
dissolve in water
gotas
drops
cada...horas
every...hours
seguir la cura hasta el final
finish the course
durante...días
for...days
inyecciones
injections
para uso externo exclusivamente
not for internal use
ungüento
ointment
aplicar/embadurnar
rub on
cucharadas (soperas/ cucharaditas)
spoonfuls (tablespoons/ tea-spoons)
tragar entero
swallow whole
tabletas
tablets
tomar/ingerir
take
estos medicamentos afectan la capacidad de conducir
this medication impairs your driving
...vez/veces cada 24 horas
...times a day

13.5 At the dentist's

Do you know a good dentist? — ¿Me podría recomendar un buen dentista?
meh pohdreeah rehkohmehndahr oon bwehn dehnteestah?

Could you make a dentist's appointment for me? It's urgent — ¿Me podría pedir hora/cita con el dentista? Es urgente
meh pohdreeah pehdeer ohrah/seetah kohn ehl dehnteestah? ehs oorhehnteh

Can I come in today, please? — ¿Me podría atender hoy mismo?
meh pohdreeah ahtehndehr oy meesmoh?

I have (terrible) toothache — Tengo (un terrible) dolor de muelas
tehngoh (oon tehrreebleh) dohlohr deh mwehlahs

Could you prescribe/ give me a painkiller? — ¿Me podría recetar/dar un analgésico?
meh pohdreeah rehsehtahr/dahr oon ahnahlhehseekoh?

Sickness 13

A piece of my tooth has broken off	Se me cayó un pedazo de un diente *seh meh kahyoh oon pehdahsoh deh oon dyehnteh*
My filling's come out	Se me salió un empaste *seh meh sahleeoh oon ehmpahsteh*
I've got a broken crown	Se me rompió la corona *seh meh ah rohmpeeoh lah kohrohnah*
I'd like/I don't want a local anaesthetic	Quisiera que/no quiero que me ponga anestesia local *keesyehrah keh/noh kyehroh keh meh pohngah ahnehstehsyah lohkahl*
Can you do a makeshift repair job?	¿Me podría hacer un arreglo provisional? *meh pohdreeah ahsehr oon ahrrehgloh prohbeesyohnahl?*
I don't want this tooth pulled	No quiero que me extraiga esta muela *noh kyehroh keh meh ehxtraheegah ehstah mwehlah*
My dentures are broken. Can you fix them?	Se me ha roto la dentadura postiza ¿Podría arreglármela? *seh meh ah rohtoh lah dehntahdoorah pohsteesah. pohdreeah arrehglahrmehlah?*

¿Qué diente/muela le duele?	Which tooth hurts?
Tiene un absceso	You've got an abscess
Tengo que tratarle el nervio	I'll have to do a root canal
Voy a ponerle anestesia local	I'm giving you a local anaesthetic
Tengo que empastarle/extraerle/pulirle este/esta...	I'll have to fill/pull this tooth/file this...down
Tengo que usar el torno	I'll have to drill
Abra la boca	Open wide, please
Cierre la boca	Close your mouth, please
Enjuáguese	Rinse, please
¿Le sigue doliendo?	Does it hurt still?

14 In trouble

14 In trouble

14.1 Asking for help

Help!	¡Socorro! *sohkohrroh!*
Fire!	¡Fuego! *fwehgoh!*
Police!	¡Policía! *pohleeseeah!*
Quick!	¡Rápido! *rahpeedoh!*
Danger!	¡Peligro! *pehleegroh!*
Watch out!	¡Cuidado! *kweedahdoh!*
Stop!	¡Alto! *ahltoh!*
Be careful!	¡Cuidado! *kweedahdoh!*
Don't!	¡No, no! *noh, noh!*
Let go!	¡Suelte! *swehlteh!*
Stop that thief!	¡Al ladrón! *ahl lahdrohn!*
Could you help me, please?	¿Podría ayudarme, por favor? *pohdreeah ahyoodahrmeh, pohr fahbohr?*
Where's the police station/emergency exit/fire escape?	¿Dónde está la comisaría/la salida de emergencia/la escalera de incendios? *dohndeh ehstah lah kohmeesahreeah/lah sahleedah deh ehmehrhehnsyah/lah ehskahlehrah deh eensehndyohs?*
Where's the nearest fire extinguisher?	¿Dónde hay un extintor? *dohndeh ay oon ehxteentohr?*
Call the fire brigade!	¡Llamen a los bomberos! *lyahmehn ah lohs bohmbehrohs!*
Call the police!	¡Llamen a la policía! *lyahmehn ah lah pohleeseeah!*
Call an ambulance!	¡Llamen a una ambulancia! *lyahmehn ah oonah ahmboolahnsyah!*
Where's the nearest phone?	¿Dónde hay un teléfono? *dohndeh ay oon tehlehfohnoh?*
Could I use your phone?	¿Podría llamar por teléfono? *pohdreeah lyahmahr pohr tehlehfohnoh?*
What's the emergency number?	¿Cuál es el número de urgencias? *kwahl ehs ehl noomehroh deh oorhehnsyahs?*
What's the number for the police?	¿Cuál es el número de la policía? *kwahl ehs ehl noomehroh deh lah pohleeseeah?*

14.2 Loss

I've lost my purse/wallet	Se me perdió el monedero/la cartera *seh meh pehrdeeoh ehl mohnehdehroh/lah kahrtehrah*
I left my...behind yesterday	Ayer dejé el/la... *ahyehr dehheh ehl/lah...*
I left my...here	Dejé el/la...aquí *dehheh ehl/lah...ahkee*
Did you find my...?	¿Encontraron mi...? *ehnkohntrahrohn mee...?*
It was right here	Estaba aquí *ehstahbah ahkee*
It's quite valuable	Es muy valioso *ehs mwee bahlyohsoh*
Where's the lost property office?	¿Dónde está la oficina de objetos perdidos? *dohndeh ehstah lah ohfeeseenah deh ohbhehtohs pehrdeedohs?*

14.3 Accidents

There's been an accident	Ha habido un accidente *ah ahbeedoh oon ahkseedehnteh*
Someone's fallen into the water	Se cayó alguien al agua *seh kahyoh ahlghyehn ahl ahgwah*
There's a fire	Hay un incendio *ay oon eensehndyoh*
Is anyone hurt?	¿Hay algún herido? *ay ahlgoon ehreedoh?*
Some people have been/no one's been injured	(No) hay heridos *(noh) ay ehreedohs*
There's someone in the car/train still	Todavía queda alguien en el carro/tren *tohdahbeeah kehdah ahlguyehn ehn ehl kahrroh/trehn*
It's not too bad. Don't worry	No es grave. No se preocupe *noh ehs grahbeh. noh seh prehohkoopeh*
Leave everything the way it is, please	No toque nada *noh tohkeh nahdah*
I want to talk to the police first	Primero quisiera hablar con la policía *preemehroh keesyehrah ahblahr kohn lah pohleeseeah*
I want to take a photo first	Primero quisiera sacar una foto *preemehroh keesyehrah sahkahr oonah fohtoh*
Here's my name and address	Aquí tiene mi nombre y dirección *ahkee tyehneh mee nohmbreh ee deerehksyohn*
Could I have your name and address?	¿Me da su nombre y dirección? *meh dah soo nohmbreh ee deerehksyohn?*
Could I see some identification/your insurance papers?	¿Me permite su carnet de identidad/sus papeles del seguro? *meh pehrmeeteh soo kahrneh deh eedehnteedah/soos pahpehlehs dehl sehgooroh?*

Will you act as a witness?	¿Puede hacer de testigo? *pwehdeh ahsehr deh tehsteegoh?*
I need the details for the insurance	Necesito los datos para el seguro *nehsehseetoh lohs dahtohs pahrah ehl sehgooroh*
Are you insured?	¿Está asegurado? *ehstah ahsehgoorahdoh?*
Third party or comprehensive?	¿Responsabilidad civil o contra todo riesgo? *rehspohnsahbeeleedahdh seebeel oh kohntrah tohdoh ryehsgoh?*
Could you sign here, please?	Firme aquí, por favor *feermeh ahkee, pohr fahbohr*

14.4 Theft

I've been robbed	Me robaron *meh rohbahrohn*
My...has been stolen	Me robaron el/la... *meh rohbahrohn ehl/lah...*
My car's been broken into	Me abrieron el carro/auto/coche *meh ahbreeyehrohn ehl kahrroh/ahootoh/kohcheh*

14.5 Missing person

I've lost my child/grandmother	Se perdió mi hijo/mi hija/mi abuela *seh pehrdeeoh mee eehoh/mee eehah/mee ahbwehlah*
Could you help me find him/her?	¿Podría ayudarme a buscarlo/la? *pohdreeah ahyoodahrmeh ah booskahrloh/lah?*
Have you seen a small child?	¿Ha visto a un niño pequeño/a una niña pequeña? *ah beestoh ah oon neenyoh pehkehnyoh/ah oonah neenyah pehkehnyah?*
He's/she's...years old	Tiene...años *tyehneh...ahnyohs*
He's/she's got short/long/blond/red/brown/black/ grey/curly/straight/frizzy hair	Tiene el pelo corto/largo/rubio/rojo/castaño/negro/ canoso/rizado/liso/crespo *tyehneh ehl pehloh kohrtoh/lahrgoh/roobyoh/kahstahnyoh/nehgroh/kahnohsoh/reesahdoh/leesoh/krehspoh*
with a ponytail	con cola de caballo *kohn kohlah deh kahbahlyoh*
with plaits	con trenzas *kohn trehnsahs*
in a bun	con moño rodete *kohn mohnyoh rohdehteh*
He's/she's got blue/brown/green eyes	Tiene ojos azules/marrones/verdes *tyehneh ohhohs ahsoolehs/mahrrohnehs/behrdehs*
He's wearing swimming trunks/mountaineering boots	Lleva bañador/botas de montaña *lyehbah bahnyahdohr/bohtahs deh mohntahnyah*
with/without glasses/a bag	con/sin gafas/bolso *kohn/seen gahfahs/bohlsoh*

tall/short — alto/bajito
ahltoh/bahheetoh

This is a photo of him/her — Esta es su foto
ehstah ehs soo fohtoh

He/she must be lost — Seguramente se habrá perdido
sehgoorahmehnteh seh ahbrah pehrdeedoh

14.6 The police

An arrest

Los papeles del carro/auto/coche, por favor — Your registration papers, please

Conducía demasiado rápido — You were speeding

Tiene mal estacionado el coche — You're not allowed to park here

No ha puesto monedas en el parquímetro — You haven't put money in the meter

No le funcionan los faros — Your lights aren't working

Le vamos a poner una multa de... pesos — That's a...peso fine

¿Va a pagar la multa en el acto? — Do you want to pay on the spot?

Tiene que pagar en el acto — You'll have to pay on the spot

I don't speak Spanish — No hablo español
noh ahbloh ehspahnyohl

I didn't see the sign — No vi el cartel
noh bee ehl kahrtehl

I don't understand what it says — No entiendo lo que dice
noh ehntyehndoh loh keh deeseh

I was only doing... kilometres an hour — Sólo iba a...kilómetros por hora
sohloh eebah ah...keelohmehtrohs pohr ohrah

I'll have my car checked — Haré revisar el carro/auto/coche
ahreh rehbeesahr ehl kahrroh/ahootoh/kohcheh

I was blinded by oncoming lights — Me cegó/encandiló un carro/auto/coche que venía de frente
meh sehgoh/ehnkahndeeloh oon kahrroh/ahootoh/kohcheh keh behneeah deh frehnteh

At the police station

I want to report a collision/missing person/rape — Vengo a hacer la denuncia de un choque/un extravío/una violación
behngoh ah ahsehr lah dehnoonsyah deh oon chohkeh/oon ehxtrahbeeoh/oonah beeohlahsyohn

Could you make out a report, please? — ¿Podría hacer un atestado/declaración?
pohdreeah ahsehr oon ahtehstahdoh/dehklahrahsyohn?

Could I have a copy for the insurance? — ¿Me podría dar una copia para el seguro?
meh pohdreeah dahr oonah kohpyah pahrah ehl sehgooroh?

I've lost everything	He perdido todo *eh pehrdeedoh tohdoh*
I'd like an interpreter	Quisiera un intérprete *keesyehrah oon eentehrprehteh*
I'm innocent	Soy inocente *soy eenohsehnteh*

¿Dónde fue?	Where did it happen?
¿Qué se le perdió?	What's missing?
¿Qué le robaron?	What's been taken?
¿Me permite su documento de identidad?	Could I see some identification?
¿A qué hora ocurrió?	What time did it happen?
¿Quiénes estuvieron implicados?	Who was involved?
¿Hay testigos?	Are there any witnesses?
Rellene este formulario	Fill this out, please
Firme aquí, por favor	Sign here, please
¿Quiere un intérprete?	Do you want an interpreter?

I don't know anything about it	No sé nada *noh seh nahdah*
I want to speak to someone...	Quisiera hablar con alguien de... *keesyehrah ahblahr kohn ahlguyehn deh...*
from the British consulate	Quisiera hablar con alguien del Consulado Británico *keesyehrah ahblahr kohn ahlguyehn dehl kohnsoolahdoh breetahneekoh*
I need to see someone from the British embassy	Quisiera hablar con alguien de la Embajada Británica *keesyehrah ahblahr kohn ahlguyehn deh lah ehmbahhahdah breetahneekah*
I want a lawyer who speaks English	Quisiera un abogado que hable inglés *keesyehrah oon ahbohgahdoh keh ahbleh eenghlehs*

15

Word list

Word list English - Spanish

This word list is meant to supplement the previous chapters. Nouns are always accompanied by the Spanish definite article in order to indicate whether it is a masculine (el) or feminine (la) word.
In a number of cases, words not contained in this list can be found elsewhere in this booklet, namely alongside the diagrams of the car, the bicycle and the tent. Many food terms can be found in the Spanish-English list in 4.7.

A

a little	un poco	*oon pohkoh*
above (up)	arriba	*ahrreebah*
abroad	el extranjero	*ehl ehxtrahnhehroh*
accident	el accidente	*ehl ahkseedehnteh*
adder	la víbora	*la veebohrah*
addition	la suma	*lah soomah*
address	la dirección	*lah deerehksyohn*
admission	la entrada	*lah ehntrahdah*
admission price	el precio de entrada	*ehl prehsyoh deh ehntrahdah*
admission ticket	la entrada	*lah ehntrahdah*
advice	el consejo	*ehl kohnsehhoh*
after	después de	*dehspwehs deh*
afternoon (in the)	(por) la tarde	*(pohr) lah tahrdeh*
aftershave	la loción para después de afeitarse	*lah lohthyohn pahrah dehspwehs deh ahfehytahrseh*
again	de nuevo	*deh nwehboh*
against	contra	*kohntrah*
age	la edad	*lah ehdahdh*
Aids	el Sida	*ehl seedah*
air conditioning	el aire acondicionado	*ehl ayreh ahkohndeesyohnahdoh*
air mattress	el colchón neumático	*ehl kohlchohn nehoomahteekoh*
air sickness bag	bolsita para el mareo	*bohlseetah pahrah ehl mahrehoh*
aircraft	el avión	*ehl ahbyohn*
airport	el aeropuerto	*ehl ahehrohpwehrtoh*
alarm	la alarma	*lah ahlahrmah*
alarm clock	el despertador	*ehl dehspehrtahdohr*
alcohol	el alcohol	*ehl ahlkohohl*
all the time	cada vez	*kahdah behs*
allergic	alérgico	*ahlehrheekoh*
alone	solo	*sohloh*
always	siempre	*syehmpreh*
ambulance	la ambulancia	*lah ahmboolahnsyah*
amount	el importe	*ehl eempohrteh*
amusement park	el parque de atracciones	*ehl pahrkeh deh ahtrahkthyohnehs*
anaesthetize	anestesiar	*ahnehstehsyahr*
anchovy	la anchoa	*lah ahnchohah*
angry	enojado	*ehnohhdahdoh*
animal	el animal	*ehl ahneemahl*
ankle	el tobillo	*ehl tohbeelyoh*
answer	la respuesta	*lah rehspwehstah*

ant	la hormiga	*lah ohrmeegah*
antibiotics	los antibióticos	*lohs ahnteebyohteekohs*
antifreeze	el anticongelante	*ehl ahnteekohnhehlahnteh*
antique	antiguo	*ahnteegwoh*
antiques	las antigüedades	*lahs ahnteegwehdahdehs*
anus	el ano	*ehl ahnoh*
apartment	el departamento	*ehl dehpahrtahmehntoh*
aperitif	el aperitivo	*ehl ahpehreeteeboh*
apologies	las disculpas	*lahs deeskoolpahs*
apple	la manzana	*lah mahnsahnah*
apple juice	el jugo de manzana	*ehl hoogoh deh mahnsahnah*
apple pie	la tarta de manzana	*lah tahrtah deh mahnsahnah*
apple sauce	el puré de manzanas	*ehl pooreh deh mahnsahnahs*
appointment	la cita	*lah seetah*
approximately	más o menos	*mahs oh mehnohs*
April	abril	*ahbreel*
archbishop	el arzobispo	*ehl ahrsohbeespoh*
architecture	la arquitectura	*lah ahrkeetehktoorah*
area	los alrededores	*lohs ahlrehdehdohrehs*
arm	el brazo	*ehl brahsoh*
arrange to meet	quedar	*kehdahr*
arrive	llegar	*lyehgahr*
arrow	la flecha	*lah flehchah*
art	el arte	*ehl ahrteh*
artery	la arteria	*lah ahrtehryah*
artichokes	las alcachofas	*lahs ahlkahchohfahs*
article	el artículo	*ehl ahrteekooloh*
artificial respiration	la respiración artificial	*lah rehspeerahsyohn ahrteefeesyahl*
arts and crafts	la artesanía	*lah ahrtehsahneeah*
ashtray	el cenicero	*ehl sehneesehroh*
ask (a question)	preguntar	*prehgoontahr*
ask for	pedir	*pehdeer*
asparagus	los espárragos	*lohs ehspahrrahgohs*
aspirin	la aspirina	*lah ahspeereenah*
assault	la agresión	*lah ahgrehsyohn*
aubergine	la berenjena	*lah behrehnhehnah*
August	agosto	*ahgohstoh*
automatic	automático	*ahootohmahteekoh*
automatic car	el carro/auto/coche con cambio automático	*ehl kahrroh/ahootoh/ kohcheh/ kohn kahmbyoh ahootohmahteekoh*
autumn	el otoño	*ehl ohtohnyoh*
avalanche	el alud	*ehl ahloodh*
awake (adj.)	despierto	*dehspyehrtoh*
awning	el toldo	*ehl tohldoh*

B

baby	el bebé	*ehl behbeh*
baby food	la comida para bebés	*lah kohmeedah pahrah behbehs*

babysitter	la niñera	*lah neenyehrah*
back (at the)	atrás	*ahtrahs*
back	la espalda	*lah ehspahldah*
backpack	la mochila	*lah mohcheelah*
bacon	el tocino	*ehl tohseenoh*
bad	mal, malo	*mahl, mahloh*
bag	la bolsa	*lah bohlsah*
baker	la panadería	*lah pahnahdehreeah*
balcony (theatre)	el palco (alto)	*ehl pahlkoh (ahltoh)*
balcony (to building)	el balcón	*ehl bahlkohn*
ball	la pelota	*lah pehlohtah*
ballet	el ballet	*ehl bahleh*
ballpoint pen	el bolígrafo	*ehl bohleegrahfoh*
banana	el plátano/la banana	*ehl plahtahnoh/ lah bahnahnah*
bandage	la gasa	*lah gahsah*
bank (river)	la orilla	*lah ohreelyah*
bank	el banco	*ehl bahnkoh*
bank card	la tarjeta del banco	*lah tahrhehtah dehl bahnkoh*
bar (café)	el bar	*ehl bahr*
bar (drinks' cabinet)	el bar	*ehl bahr*
bar	la barra	*lah bahrrah*
barbecue	la barbacoa	*lah bahrbahkohah*
basketball	el baloncesto	*ehl bahlohnsehstoh*
bath	el baño	*ehl bahnyoh*
bath attendant	el bañista	*ehl bahnyeestah*
bath foam	el gel de baño	*ehl hehl deh bahnyoh*
bath towel	la toalla de baño	*lah tohahlyah deh bahnyoh*
bathing cap	el gorro de baño	*ehl gohrroh deh bahnyoh*
bathing cubicle	la caseta	*lah kahsehtah*
bathing suit	el bañador	*ehl bahnyahdohr*
bathroom	el cuarto de baño	*ehl kwahrtoh deh bahnyoh*
battery (car)	la batería	*lah bahtehreeah*
battery	la pila	*lah peelah*
beach	la playa	*lah plahyah*
beans	los frijoles/porotos blancos	*lohs freehohlehs/ pohrohtohs blahnkohs*
beautiful	bonito/lindo	*bohneetoh/leendoh*
beauty parlour	el salón de belleza	*ehl sahlohn deh behlyehsah*
bed	la cama	*lah kahmah*
bee	la abeja	*lah ahbehhah*
beef	la carne de vaca	*lah kahrneh deh bahkah*
beer	la cerveza	*lah sehrbehsah*
beetroot	la remolacha	*lah rehmohlahchah*
begin	empezar	*ehmpehsahr*
beginner	el principiante	*ehl preenseepyahnteh*
behind	atrás	*ahtrahs*
Belgian (f)	la belga	*lah behlgah*
Belgian (m)	el belga	*ehl behlgah*
Belgium	Bélgica	*behlheekah*
bellboy	el mozo de cuerda/ botones	*ehl mohsoh deh kwehrdah/bohtohnehs*

belt	el cinturón	*ehl seentoorohn*
berth	la litera	*lah leetehrah*
better	mejor	*mehhohr*
bicarb	el bicarbonato	*ehl beekahrbohnahtoh*
bicycle	la bicicleta	*lah beeseeklehtah*
bicycle pump	el inflador	*ehl eenflahdohr*
bicycle repairman	el mecánico de bicicletas	*ehl mehkahneekoh deh beeseeklehtahs*
bikini	el/la bikini	*ehl/lah beekeenee*
bill	la cuenta	*lah kwehntah*
billiards, to play	el juego de billar	*ehl hwehgoh deh beelyahr*
birthday (to have a)	cumplir años	*koompleer ahnyohs*
birthday	el cumpleaños	*ehl koomplehahnyohs*
biscuit	la galleta	*lah gahlyehtah*
bite	morder	*mohrdehr*
bitter	amargo	*ahmahrgoh*
black	negro	*nehgroh*
bland	soso/desabrido	*sohsoh/dehsahbreedoh*
blanket	la manta/frazada	*lah mahntah/frahsahdah*
bleach	teñir de rubio	*tehnyeer deh roobyoh*
blister	la ampolla	*lah ahmpohlyah*
blond	rubio	*roobyoh*
blood	la sangre	*lah sahngreh*
blood pressure	la tensión/presión sanguínea	*lah tehnsyohn/prehsyohn sahngheenehah*
blouse	la blusa	*lah bloosah*
blow dry	secar a mano	*sehkahr ah mahnoh*
blue	azul	*ahsool*
boat	el barco	*ehl bahrkoh*
body	el cuerpo	*ehl kwehrpoh*
body milk	la leche corporal	*lah lehcheh kohrpohrahl*
boiled	cocido	*kohseedoh*
boiled ham	el jamón de York/cocido	*ehl hahmohn deh yohrk/kohseedoh*
bonbon	el bombón	*ehl bohmbohn*
bone	el hueso	*ehl wehsoh*
bonnet	el capó	*ehl kahpoh*
book (verb)	reservar	*rehsehrbahr*
book	el libro	*ehl leebroh*
booked	reservado	*rehsehrbahdah*
booking office	la taquilla	*lah tahkeelyah*
bookshop	la librería	*lah leebrehreeah*
border	la frontera	*lah frohntehrah*
bored (be)	aburrirse	*ahboorreerseh*
boring	aburrido	*ahboorreedoh*
born	nacido	*nahseedoh*
botanical gardens	el jardín botánico	*ehl hahrdeen bohtahneekoh*
both	ambos/ambas	*ahmbohs/ahmbahs*
bottle (baby's)	el biberón	*ehl beebehrohn*
bottle	la botella	*lah bohtehlyah*
bottle-warmer	el calentador de biberones	*ehl kahlehntahdohr de beebehrohnehs*
box (in theatre)	el palco	*ehl pahlkoh*
box	la caja	*kahhah*
boy	el chico	*ehl cheekoh*

bra	el sujetador	*ehl soohehtahdohr*
bracelet	la pulsera	*lah poolsehrah*
braised	estofado	*ehstohfahdoh*
brake	el freno	*ehl frehnoh*
brake fluid	el líquido de frenos	*ehl leekeedoh deh frehnohs*
bread	el pan	*ehl pahn*
breakdown recovery	el auxilio en carretera	*ehl ahooxeelyoh ehn kahrrehtehrah*
break (limb)	fracturarse	*frahktoorahrseh*
breakfast	el desayuno	*ehl dehsahyoonoh*
breast	el pecho	*ehl pehchoh*
bridge	el puente	*ehl pwehnteh*
bring	llevar	*lyehbahr*
brochure	el folleto	*ehl fohlyehtoh*
broken	roto, estropeado	*rohtoh, ehstrohpehahdoh*
broth	el caldo	*ehl kahldoh*
brother	el hermano	*ehl ehrmahnoh*
brown	marrón	*mahrrohn*
bruise (verb)	contusionarse	*kohntoosyohnahrseh*
brush	el cepillo	*ehl sehpeelyoh*
Brussels sprouts	las coles de Bruselas	*lahs kohlehs deh broosehlahs*
bucket	el cubo/el balde	*ehl kooboh/ehl bahldeh*
bug	el bicho	*ehl beechoh*
building	el edificio	*ehl ehdeefeesyoh*
bullfight	la corrida de toros	*lah kohrreedah deh tohrohs*
buoy	la boya	*lah boyah*
burglary	el robo en una casa	*ehl rohboh ehn oonah kahsah*
burn (verb)	quemar	*kehmahr*
burn	la quemadura	*lah kehmahdoorah*
burnt	quemado	*kehmahdoh*
bus	el autobús/ el camión/ el omnibús	*ehl ahootohboos/ ehl kahmyohn/ ehl ohmneeboos*
bus station	la estación de autobuses	*lah ehstahthyohn deh ahootohboosehs*
bus stop	la parada de autobús	*lah pahrahdah deh ahootohboosehs*
business class	la clase preferente	*lah klahseh prehfehrehnteh*
business trip	el viaje de negocios	*ehl byahheh deh nehgohsyohs*
busy (crowded)	hay mucha gente	*ay moochah hehnteh*
butane camping gas	el gas butano	*ehl gahs bootahnoh*
butcher's	la carnicería	*lah kahrneesehreeah*
butter	la mantequilla	*lah mahntehkeelyah*
button	el botón	*ehl bohtohn*
buy	comprar	*kohmprahr*
by airmail	el correo aéreo/ vía aérea	*ehl kohrrehoh ahehrehoh/beeah ahehrehah*

C

cabbage	la col, la berza	*lah kohl, lah behrthah*
cabin	la cabaña	*lah kahbahnyah*
cake	el pastel/queque	*ehl pahstehl/kehkeh*
cake shop	la pastelería, la confitería	*lah pahstehlehreeah, lah kohnfeetehreeah*
call (by phone)	llamar por teléfono	*lyahmahr pohr tehlehfohnoh*
called, to be	llamarse	*lyahmahrseh*
camera	la máquina/cámara fotográfica	*lah mahkeenah/ kahmahrah fohtohgrahfeekah*
camp	acampar	*ahkahmpahr*
camp shop	la tienda del camping	*lah tyehndah dehl kahmpeen*
camp site	el camping	*ehl kahmpeen*
camper van	el autocaravana	*ehl ahootohkahrah-bahnah*
campfire	la fogata	*lah fohgahtah*
camping guide	la guía de camping	*lah gheeah deh kahmpeen*
camping permit	el permiso de acampar	*ehl pehrmeesoh deh ahkahmpahr*
canal boat	el barco de excursión	*ehl bahrkoh deh ehxkoorsyohn*
cancel	cancelar	*kahnsehlahr*
candle	la vela	*lah behlah*
canoe	la canoa	*lah kahnohah*
canoeing	el piragüismo	*ehl peerahgweesmoh*
cap (hat)	el gorro	*ehl gohrroh*
car	el carro/auto/coche	*ehl kahrroh/ahootoh/ kohcheh*
car deck	la bodega para carros/autos/coches	*lah bohdehgah pahrah kahrrohs/ahootohs/ kohchehs*
car documents	los papeles del carro/auto	*lohs pahpehlehs dehl kahrroh/ahootoh*
car registration	el permiso de circulación	*ehl pehrmeesoh deh seerkoolahsyohn*
car trouble	la avería	*lah ahbehreeah*
carafe	la jarra	*lah hahrrah*
caravan	la caravana casa rodante	*lah kahrahbahnah kahsah rohdahnteh*
cardigan	el chaleco	*ehl chahlehkoh*
careful	con cuidado	*kohn kweedahdoh*
carrot	la zanahoria	*lah sahnahohryah*
carton	el cartón	*ehl kahrtohn*
cartridge	el carrete de cassette	*ehl kahrrehteh deh kahseht*
cascade	la cascada	*lah kahskahdah*
cash desk	la caja	*lah kahhah*
casino	el casino	*ehl kahseenoh*
cassette	el cassette	*ehl kahseht*
castle	el castillo	*ehl kahsteelyoh*
cat	el gato	*ehl gahtoh*
catalogue	el catálogo	*ehl kahtahlohgoh*
cathedral	la catedral	*lah kahtehdrahl*

cauliflower	la coliflor	*lah kohleeflohr*
cave	la gruta	*lah grootah*
CD	el compact disc	*ehl kohmpahkt deesk*
celebrate	celebrar una fiesta	*sehlehbrahr oonah fyehstah*
cellotape	la cinta adhesiva	*lah seentah ahdehseebah*
cemetery	el cementerio	*ehl sehmehntehryoh*
centimetre	centímetro(s)	*sehnteemehtroh(s)*
central heating	la calefacción central	*lah kahlehfaksyohn sehntrahl*
centre (in the)	en el centro/medio	*ehn ehl sehntroh/ mehdyoh*
centre	el centro	*ehl sehntroh*
chair	la silla	*lah seelyah*
chambermaid	la camarera	*lah kahmahrehrah*
chamois	la gamuza	*lah gahmoosah*
champagne	el champán/el cava	*ehl chahmpahn/ehl kahbah*
change (from paying)	el vuelto	*ehl bwehltoh*
change (train/plane etc.)	hacer trasbordo	*ahsehr trahsbohrdoh*
change (verb)	cambiar	*kahmbyahr*
change the baby's nappy	cambiar los pañales	*kahmbyahr lohs pahnyahlehs*
change the oil	cambiar el aceite	*kahmbyahr ehl ahseyteh*
chapel	la capilla	*lah kahpeelyah*
charter flight	el vuelo chárter	*ehl bwehloh chahrtehr*
chat up	ligar/levantar	*leegahr/lehbahntar*
check (verb)	controlar	*kohntrohlahr*
check in	facturar	*fahktoorahr*
cheers	salud	*sahloodh*
cheese (tasty, mild)	el queso (añejo, blando)	*ehl kehsoh (ahnyehhoh, blahndoh)*
chef	el jefe/chef	*ehl hehfeh/chehf*
chemist	la farmacia	*lah fahrmahsyah*
cheque	el cheque	*ehl chehkeh*
cherries	las cerezas	*lahs sehrehsahs*
chess (play)	jugar al ajedrez	*hoogahr ahl ahehdres*
chewing gum	el chicle	*ehl cheekleh*
chicken	el pollo	*ehl pohlyoh*
chicory	las endivias	*lahs ehndeebyahs*
child	el hijo, el niño	*ehl eehoh, ehl neenyoh*
child seat	el asiento para niños	*ehl ahsyehntoh pahrah neenyohs*
child's seat	la silla para niños	*lah seelyah pahrah neenyohs*
chilled	refrigerado	*rehfreehehrahdoh*
chin	la barbilla	*lah bahrbeelyah*
chips/crisps	las patatas/papas fritas	*lahs pahtahtahs/ pahpahs freetahs*
chocolate	el chocolate	*ehl chohkohlahteh*
choose	elegir/escoger	*ehlehheer/ehskohhehr*
chop	la chuleta	*la choolehtah*
christian name	el nombre	*ehl nohmbreh*
church	la iglesia	*lah eeglehsyah*

church service	el servicio religioso	*ehl sehrbeesyoh rehleehyohsoh*
cigar	el puro	*ehl pooroh*
cigarette	el cigarro	*ehl seegahrroh*
cigarette paper	el papel de fumar	*ehl pahpehl deh foomahr*
cine camera	la filmadora	*lah feelmahdohrah*
circle	el círculo	*ehl seerkooloh*
circus	el circo	*ehl seerkoh*
city map	el plano	*ehl plahnoh*
classic/classical	clásica	*klahseekah*
clean (adj.)	limpio	*leempyoh*
clean (verb)	limpiar	*leempyahr*
clear (adj.)	claro	*klahroh*
clearance	la liquidación	*lah leekeedahsyohn*
closed	cerrado	*sehrrahdoh*
closed off	(la carretera) cerrada	*(lah kahrrehtehrah) sehrrahdah*
clothes	la ropa	*lah rohpah*
clothes hanger	la percha	*lah pehrchah*
clothes peg	la pinza/el broche para la ropa	*lah peensah/ehl brohcheh pahrah lah rohpah*
coat	el abrigo	*ehl ahbreegoh*
cockroach	la cucaracha	*lah kookahrahchah*
cod	el bacalao (fresco)	*ehl bahkahlahoh (frehskoh)*
coffee	el café	*ehl kahfeh*
coffee creamer	la crema para el café	*lah krehmah pahrah ehl kahfeh*
coffee filter	el filtro de café	*ehl feeltroh deh kahfeh*
cognac	el coñac	*ehl kohnyakh*
cold	frío	*freeoh*
cold	el resfrío	*ehl rehsfreeoh*
cold cuts	los fiambres	*lohs fyahmbrehs*
collarbone	la clavícula	*lah klahbeekoolah*
colleague	el/la colega	*ehl/lah kohlehgah*
collision	el choque	*ehl chohkeh*
cologne	el agua de tocador	*ehl ahgwah deh tohkahdohr*
colour	el color	*ehl kohlohr*
colour TV	el televisor de color	*ehl tehlehbeesohr deh kohlohr*
coloured pencils	los lápices de colores	*lohs lahpeesehs deh kohlohrehs*
colouring book	el libro para colorear	*ehl leebroh pahrah kohlohrehahr*
comb	el peine	*ehl peheeneh*
come	venir	*behneer*
compartment	el compartimiento	*ehl kohmpahrteemyehntoh*
complaint (medical)	la molestia	*lah mohlehstyah*
complaint	la queja	*lah kehhah*
complaints book	el libro de quejas	*ehl leebroh deh kehhahs*
completely	del todo	*dehl tohdoh*
compliment	el cumplido	*ehl koompleedoh*
compulsory	obligatorio	*ohbleegahtohryoh*

concert	el concierto	*ehl kohnsyehrtoh*
concert hall	la sala de conciertos	*lah sahlah deh kohnsyehrtohs*
concussion	la conmoción cerebral	*lah kohnmohsyohn sehrehbrahl*
condiments	los condimentos	*lohs kohndeemehntohs*
condom	el condón	*ehl kohndohn*
congratulate	felicitar	*fehleeseetahr*
connection	el enlace	*ehl ehnlahseh*
constipation	el estreñimiento	*ehl ehstrehnyeemyehntoh*
consulate	el consulado	*ehl kohnsoolahdoh*
consultation	la consulta	*lah kohnsooltah*
contact lens	la lentilla/el lente de contacto	*lah lehnteelyah/ehl lehnteh deh kohntahktoh*
contact lens solution	el líquido para las lentillas	*ehl leekeedoh pahrah lahs lehnteelyahs*
contagious	contagioso	*kohntahhyohsoh*
contest	el concurso	*ehl kohnkoorsoh*
contraceptive	el anticonceptivo	*ehl ahnteekohn-sehpteeboh*
contraceptive pill	la píldora anticonceptiva	*lah peeldohrah ahnteekohnsehpteebah*
convent	el convento	*ehl kohnbehntoh*
cook (verb)	cocinar	*kohseenahr*
cook	el cocinero	*ehl kohseenehroh*
copper	el cobre	*ehl kohbreh*
copy	la copia	*lah kohpyah*
corkscrew	el sacacorchos	*ehl sahkahkohrchohs*
corn flour	la maicena	*lah maheesehnah*
corner	el rincón	*ehl reenkohn*
correct	correcto	*kohrrehktoh*
correspond	cartearse	*kahrtehahrseh*
corridor	el pasillo	*ehl pahseelyoh*
costume	el traje	*ehl trahheh*
cot	la cuna	*lah koonah*
cotton	el algodón	*ehl ahlgohdohn*
cotton wool	el algodón	*ehl ahlgohdohn*
cough	la tos	*lah tohs*
cough mixture	el jarabe para la tos	*ehl hahrahbeh pahrah lah tohs*
counter	el mostrador	*ehl mohstrahdohr*
country	el país	*ehl pahees*
country code	el indicativo del país	*ehl eendeekahteeboh dehl pahees*
country(side)	el campo	*ehl kahmpoh*
courgette	el calabacín	*ehl kahlahbahseen*
course (of treatment)	la cura	*lah koorah*
cousin (f)	la prima	*lah preemah*
cousin (m)	el primo	*ehl preemoh*
crab	el cangrejo	*ehl kahngrehoh*
cream	la crema, la nata	*lah krehmah, lah nahtah*
credit card	la tarjeta de crédito	*lah tahr_ehtah deh krehdeetoh*
crisps/chips	las patatas fritas	*lahs pahtahtahs freetahs*
croissant	el croissant	*ehl krwahsahn*
cross the road	cruzar la calle	*kroosahr lah kahlyeh*

cross-country run	la pista de esquí de fondo	*lah peestah deh ehskee deh fohndoh*
cross-country skiing	el esquí de fondo	*ehl ehskee deh fohndoh*
cross-country skis	los esquís de fondo	*lohs ehskees deh fohndoh*
crossing (journey)	la travesía	*lah trahbehseeah*
cry (verb)	llorar	*lyohrahr*
cubic metre(s)	metro(s) cúbico(s)	*mehtroh(s) koobeekoh(s)*
cucumber	el pepino	*ehl pehpeenoh*
cuddly toy	el animal de peluche	*ehl ahneemahl deh pehloocheh*
cuff links	los gemelos/ las mancuernas	*lohs hehmehlohs/ lahs mahnkwehrnahs*
culottes	la falda-pantalón	*lah fahldah pahntahlohn*
cup	la taza	*lah tahsah*
curly	rizado	*reesahdoh*
current	la corriente	*lah kohrryehnteh*
cushion	el cojín	*ehl cohheen*
custard	las natillas/el flan	*lahs nahteelyahs/ ehl flahn*
customary	habitual	*ahbeetwahl*
customs	la aduana	*lah ahdwahna*
customs check	el control de aduanas	*ehl kohntrohl deh ahdwahnahs*
cut (verb)	cortar	*kohrtahr*
cutlery	los cubiertos	*lohs koobyehrtohs*
cycling	andar en bicicleta	*ahndahr ehn beeseeklehtah*

D

dairy products	los productos lácteos	*lohs prohdooktohs lahktehohs*
damaged	dañado, estropeado	*dahnyahdoh, ehstrohpehahdoh*
dance	bailar	*bahylahr*
dandruff	la caspa	*lah kahspah*
danger	el peligro	*ehl pehleegroh*
dangerous	peligroso	*pehleegrohsoh*
dark	oscuro	*ohskooroh*
date	la cita	*lah seetah*
daughter	la hija	*lah eehah*
day	el día, las 24 horas	*ehl deeah, lahs beheenteekwahtroh ohrahs*
day before yesterday	anteayer	*ahntehahyehr*
dead	muerto	*mwehrtoh*
decaffeinated	sin cafeína	*seen kahfeheenah*
December	diciembre	*deesyehmbreh*
deck chair	el sillón de playa	*ehl seelyohn deh plahyah*
declare(customs)	declarar	*dehklahrahr*
deep	hondo	*ohndoh*
deep sea diving	el buceo	*ehl boosehoh*
degrees	los grados	*lohs grahdohs*
delay	el retraso	*ehl rehtrahsoh*

delicious	delicioso	*dehleesyohsoh*
dentist	el dentista	*ehl dehnteestah*
dentures	la dentadura postiza	*lah dehntahdoorah pohsteesah*
deodorant	el desodorante	*ehl dehsohdohrahnteh*
department	la sección	*lah sehksyohn*
department stores	los grandes almacenes	*lohs grahndehs ahlmahsehnehs*
departure	la partida	*lah pahrteedah*
departure time	la hora de salida	*lah ohrah deh sahleedah*
depilatory cream	la crema depilatoria	*lah krehmah dehpeelahtohryah*
deposit (in)	en consigna	*ehn kohnseegnah*
deposit	la fianza	*lah fyahnsah*
dessert	el postre	*ehl pohstreh*
destination	el destino, el punto final	*ehl dehsteenoh, ehl poontoh feenahl*
develop (photos)	revelar	*rehbehlahr*
diabetic	el diabético	*ehl dyahbehteekoh*
dial (verb)	marcar	*mahrkahr*
diamond	el diamante	*ehl deeahmahnteh*
diarrhoea	la diarrea	*lah deeahrrehah*
dictionary	el diccionario	*ehl deeksyohnahryoh*
diesel	el gasóleo/gasoil	*ehl gahsohlehoh/ gahsoheel*
diet	la dieta	*lah dyehtah*
difficulty	la dificultad	*lah deefeekooltahdh*
dining room	el comedor	*ehl kohmehdohr*
dining/buffet car	el coche restaurante	*ehl kohcheh rehstahoorahnteh*
dinner (to have)	cenar	*sehnahr*
dinner	la cena, la comida	*lah sehnah, lah kohmeedah*
dinner jacket	el smoking	*ehl ehsmohkeen*
direction	la dirección	*lah deerehksyohn*
directly	directo	*deerehktoh*
dirty	sucio	*soosyoh*
disabled person	el minusválido	*ehl meenoosbahleedoh*
disappearance	la desaparición	*lah dehsahpahree-syohn*
disco	la discoteca	*lah deeskohtehkah*
discount	el descuento	*ehl dehskwehntoh*
dish	el plato	*ehl plahtoh*
dish of the day	el plato del día	*ehl plahtoh dehl deeah*
disinfectant	el desinfectante	*ehl dehseen-fehktahnteh*
distance	la distancia	*lah deestahnsyah*
distilled water	el agua destilada	*ehl ahgwah dehsteelahdah*
disturb	molestar	*mohlehstahr*
disturbance	el fallo	*ehl fahlyoh*
dive (verb)	bucear	*boosehahr*
diving	el buceo	*ehl boosehoh*
diving board	el trampolín	*ehl trahmpohleen*
diving gear	el equipo de buzo	*ehl ehkeepoh deh boosoh*

divorced	divorciado	*deebohrsyahdoh*
DIY-shop	la tienda de artículos de bricolaje	*lah tyehndah deh ahrteekoolohs deh breekohlaheh*
dizzy	mareado	*mahrehahdoh*
do (verb)	hacer	*ahsehr*
doctor	el médico	*ehl mehdeekoh*
dog	el perro	*ehl pehrroh*
doll	la muñeca	*lah moonyehkah*
domestic	nacionales	*nahseeohnahlehs*
done	hecho	*ehchoh*
door	la puerta	*lah pwehrtah*
double	doble	*dohbleh*
down	abajo	*ahbahhoh*
draught (to be a)	haber corriente	*ahbehr kohrryehnteh*
draughts (play)	jugar a las damas	*hoogahr ah lahs dahmahs*
dream	soñar	*sohnyahr*
dress	el vestido	*ehl behsteedoh*
dressing gown	la bata	*lah bahtah*
drink (verb)	beber	*behbehr*
drinking chocolate	el chocolate	*ehl chohkohlahteh*
drinking water	el agua potable	*ehl ahgwah pohtahbleh*
drive (verb)	ir en coche	*eer ehn kohcheh*
driver	el chófer	*ehl chohfehr*
driving licence	el permiso de conducir	*ehl pehrmeesoh deh kohndooseer*
drought	la sequía	*lah sehkeeah*
dry (verb)	secar	*sehkahr*
dry	seco	*sehkoh*
dry clean	lavar en seco	*lahbahr ehn sehkoh*
dry cleaner's	la tintorería	*lah teentohrehreeah*
dry shampoo	el champú seco	*ehl chahmpoo sehkoh*
dummy	el chupete/chupón	*ehl choopehteh/ choopohn*
during	durante	*doorahnteh*
during the day	de día	*deh deeah*
E		
ear	la oreja	*lah ohrehhah*
ear, nose and throat (ENT) specialist	el médico de oídos	*ehl mehdeekoh deh oheedohs*
earache	el dolor de oído	*ehl dohlohr deh oheedoh*
eardrops	las gotas para los oídos	*lahs gohtahs pahrah lohs oheedohs*
early	temprano	*tehmprahnoh*
earrings	los pendientes/ aretes	*lohs pehndyehntehs/ ahrehtehs*
earth	la tierra	*lah tyehrrah*
earthenware	la cerámica	*lah sehrahmeekah*
east	el este	*ehl ehsteh*
easy	fácil	*fahseel*
eat	comer	*kohmehr*
eczema	el eczema	*ehl ehksehmah*
eel	la anguila	*lah ahngueelah*
egg	el huevo/blanquillo	*ehl wehboh/blahnkeelyoh*

elastic band	la goma elástica/ liga	*lah gohmah ehlahsteekah/leegah*
electric	eléctrico	*ehlehktreekoh*
electricity	la corriente	*lah kohrryehnteh*
embassy	la embajada	*lah ehmbahhahdah*
emergency brake	el freno de emergencia	*ehl frehnoh deh ehmehrhehnsyah*
emergency exit	la salida de emergencia	*lah sahleedah deh ehmehrhehnsyah*
emergency number	el número de urgencias	*ehl noomehroh deh oorhehnsyahs*
emergency phone	el teléfono de emergencia	*ehl tehlehfohnoh deh ehmehrhehnsyah*
emergency triangle	el triángulo reflectante	*ehl treeahngooloh rehflehktahnteh*
emery board	la lima (para uñas)	*lah leemah (pahrah oonyahs)*
empty	vacío	*bahseeoh*
engaged	ocupado	*ohkoopahdoh*
English	inglés	*eenglehs*
enjoy	disfrutar	*deesfrootahr*
entertainment guide	la guía de los espectáculos	*lah gheeah deh lohs ehspehktahkoolohs*
envelope	el sobre	*ehl sohbreh*
escort	el/la acompañante	*ehl/lah ahkohmpahnyahnteh*
evening	la tarde	*lah tahrdeh*
evening wear	el traje de etiqueta	*ehl trahheh deh ehteekehtah*
event	el acontecimiento	*ehl akohntehsee-myehntoh*
event (social)	la función	*lah foonsyohn*
everything	todo	*tohdoh*
everywhere	en todas partes	*ehn tohdahs pahrtehs*
examine	reconocer/ examinar	*rehkohnohsehr/ ehksahmeenahr*
excavation	las excavaciones	*lahs ehxkahbahsyohnehs*
excellent	excelente, estupendo	*ehxsehlehnteh, ehstoopehndoh*
exchange (verb)	cambiar	*kahmbyahr*
exchange office	la oficina de cambio	*lah ohfeeseenah deh kahmbyoh*
exchange rate	la cotización, el tipo de cambio	*lah kohteesahsyohn, ehl teepoh deh kahmbyoh*
excursion	la excursión organizada	*lah ehxkoorsyohn ohrgahneesahdah*
exhibition	la exposición	*lah ehxpohseesyohn*
exit	la salida	*lah sahleedah*
expenses	los gastos	*lohs gahstohs*
expensive	caro	*kahroh*
explain	explicar	*ehxpleekahr*
express train	el tren rápido	*ehl trehn rahpeedoh*
external	tópico, externo	*tohpeekoh, ehxtehrnoh*
eye	el ojo	*ehl ohhoh*
eye drops	las gotas para los ojos	*lahs gohtahs pahrah lohs ohhohs*

eye shadow	la sombra de ojos	*lah sohmbrah deh ohhohs*
eye specialist	el oculista	*ehl ohkooleestah*
eyeliner	el lápiz de ojos	*ehl lahpees deh ohhohs*

F

face	la cara	*lah kahrah*
factory	la fábrica	*lah fahbreekah*
fair	la feria	*lah fehryah*
fall	caer(se)	*kahehr(seh)*
family	la familia	*lah fahmeelyah*
famous	famoso	*fahmohsoh*
far away	lejos	*lehhohs*
farm	la granja	*lah grahnhah*
farmer	el campesino	*ehl kahmpehseenoh*
farmer's wife	la campesina	*lah kahmpehseenah*
fashion	la moda	*lah mohdah*
fast	rápido	*rahpeedoh*
father	el padre	*ehl pahdreh*
fault (blame)	la culpa	*lah koolpah*
fax (verb)	enviar un fax	*ehnbyahr oon fahx*
February	febrero	*fehbrehroh*
feel (verb)	sentir	*sehnteer*
feel like	tener ganas	*tehnehr gahnahs*
fence	la verja/cerca	*lah behrhah/sehrkah*
ferry	el transbordador	*ehl trahnsbohrdahdohr*
fever	la fiebre	*lah fyehbreh*
fill (tooth)	empastar	*ehmpahstahr*
fill out	rellenar	*rehlyehnahr*
filling	el empaste	*ehl ehmpahsteh*
film (camera)	el rollo	*ehl rohlyoh*
film	la película	*lah pehleekoolah*
filter	el filtro	*ehl feeltroh*
find (verb)	encontrar	*ehnkohntrahr*
fine	la multa	*lah mooltah*
finger	el dedo	*ehl dehdoh*
fire	el fuego	*ehl fwehgoh*
fire (house etc.)	el incendio	*ehl eensehndyoh*
fire brigade	los bomberos	*lohs bohmbehrohs*
fire escape	la escalera de incendios	*lah ehskahlehrah deh eensehndyohs*
fire extinguisher	el extintor	*ehl ehxteentohr*
first	primero	*preemehroh*
first aid	los primeros auxilios	*lohs preemehrohs ahooxeelyohs*
first class	la primera clase	*lah preemehrah klahseh*
fish (verb)	pescar	*pehskahr*
fish	el pescado	*ehl pehskahdoh*
fishing rod	la caña de pescar	*lah kanyah deh pehskahr*
fitness centre	el gimnasio	*ehl heemnahsyoh*
fitness training	la gimnasia	*lah heemnahsyah*
fitting room	el probador	*ehl prohbahdohr*
fix puncture	arreglar el pinchazo	*ahrrehglahr ehl peenchahsoh*

flag	la bandera	*lah bahndehrah*
flamenco	el flamenco	*ehl flahmehnkoh*
flash cube	el cuboflash	*ehl koobohflahsh*
flash gun/bulb	el flash	*ehl flahsh*
flat	el departamento	*ehl dehpahrtahmehntoh*
flight	el vuelo	*ehl bwehloh*
flight number	el número de vuelo	*ehl noomehroh deh bwehloh*
flood	la inundación	*lah eenoondasyohn*
floor	el piso	*ehl peesoh*
flour	la harina	*lah ahreenah*
flu	la gripe	*lah greepeh*
fly (insect)	la mosca	*lah mohskah*
fly (verb)	volar	*bohlahr*
fly-over	el viaducto	*ehl beeahdooktoh*
fog	la niebla	*lah nyehblah*
foggy (be)	haber niebla	*ahbehr nyehblah*
folkloristic	folclórico	*fohlklohreekoh*
follow	seguir	*sehgueer*
food	el alimento	*ehl ahleemehntoh*
food poisoning	la intoxicación alimenticia	*lah eentohxeekahsyohn ahleemehnteesyah*
foodstuffs	los víveres	*lohs beebehrehs*
foot	el pie	*ehl pyeh*
for	antes, delante de	*ahntehs, dehlahnteh deh*
for hire	se alquila	*seh ahlkeelah*
forbidden	prohibido	*proheebeedoh*
forehead	la frente	*lah frehnteh*
foreign	extranjero	*ehxtrahnhehroh*
forget	olvidar	*ohlbeedahr*
fork	el tenedor	*ehl tehnehdohr*
form	el formulario	*ehl fohrmoolahryoh*
fort	la fortificación	*lah fohrteefeekah-syohn*
forward (send)	enviar	*ehnbyahr*
fountain	la fuente	*lah fwehnteh*
four-star petrol	súper	*soopehr*
frame	la montura	*lah mohntoorah*
free	libre	*leebreh*
free of charge	gratuito	*grahtweetoh*
free time	el tiempo libre	*ehl tyehmpoh leebreh*
freeze	helar	*ehlahr*
French	francés	*frahnsehs*
French bread	la barra de pan	*lah bahrrah deh pahn*
fresh	fresco	*frehskoh*
Friday	el viernes	*ehl byehrnehs*
fried	frito	*freetoh*
fried egg	el huevo al plato	*ehl wehboh ahl plahtoh*
friend	el amigo	*ehl ahmeegoh*
friendly	cordial, amable	*kohrdyahl, ahmahbleh*
frightened	miedoso	*myehdohsoh*
fringe	el flequillo	*ehl flehkeelyoh*
front (at the)	adelante	*ahdehlahnteh*
frozen goods	los productos congelados	*los prohdooktohs kohnhehlahdohs*
fruit	la fruta	*lah frootah*

fruit juice	el jugo de frutas	*ehl hoogoh deh frootahs*
frying pan	la sartén	*lah sahrtehn*
full	lleno	*lyehnoh*
fun	la diversión	*lah deebehrsyohn*

G

gallery	la galería de arte	*lah gahlehreeah deh ahrteh*
game	el juego	*el hwehgoh*
garage (for repairs)	el taller mecánico	*ehl tahlyehr mehkahneekoh*
garbage bag	la bolsa de basura	*lah bohlsah deh bahsoorah*
garden	el jardín	*ehl hahrdeen*
gastroenteritis	la gastroenteritis	*lah gahstrohehnteh-reetees*
gauze	la gasa esterilizada	*lah gahsah ehstehreeleesahdah*
gear (bicycle)	el cambio	*ehl kahmbyoh*
gel	el gel	*ehl hehl*
German	alemán	*ahlehmahn*
get married	casarse	*kahsahrseh*
get off	bajarse	*bahhahrse*
gift	el regalo	*ehl rehgahloh*
gilt	dorado	*dohrahdoh*
ginger	el jengibre	*ehl hehnheebreh*
girl	la chica	*lah cheekah*
girlfriend	la amiga	*lah ahmeegah*
giro card	la tarjeta de la caja postal	*lah tahrhehtah deh lah kahhah pohstahl*
giro cheque	el cheque postal	*ehl chehkeh pohstahl*
glacier	el glaciar	*ehl glahsyahr*
glass (tumbler)	el vaso	*ehl bahsoh*
glass (wine -)	la copa	*lah kohpah*
glasses	las gafas/los lentes	*lahs gahfahs/lohs lehntes*
glider	el vuelo sin motor	*ehl bwehloh seen mohtohr*
glove	el guante	*ehl gwahnteh*
glue	la cola/el pegamento	*lah kohlah/ ehl pehgahmehntoh*
gnat	el mosquito	*ehl mohskeetoh*
go (verb)	ir	*eer*
go back, come back	volver	*bohlbehr*
go backwards	ir para atrás	*eer pahrah ahtrahs*
go out	salir	*sahleer*
goat's cheese	el queso de cabra	*ehl kehsoh deh kahbrah*
gold	el oro	*ehl ohroh*
golf	el golf	*ehl gohlf*
golf course	el campo de golf	*ehl kahmpoh deh gohlf*
gone	perdido	*pehrdeedoh*
good afternoon	buenas tardes (after 12am)	*bwehnahs tahrdehs*
good evening	buenas tardes	*bwehnahs tahrdehs*
good morning	buenos días (before 12am)	*bwehnohs deeahs*
good night	buenas noches	*bwehnahs nohchehs*

goodbye	adiós/la despedida	*ahdeeohs/ lah dehspehdeedah*
gram	el gramo	*ehl grahmoh*
grandchild	el nieto	*ehl nyehtoh*
grandfather	el abuelo	*ehl ahbwehloh*
grandmother	la abuela	*lah ahbwehlah*
grape juice	el jugo de uvas	*ehl hoogoh deh oobahs*
grapefruit	el pomelo/la toronja	*ehl pohmehloh/ lah tohrohnhah*
grapes	las uvas	*lahs oobahs*
grave	la tumba	*lah toombah*
grease	la grasa	*lah grahsah*
green	verde	*behrdeh*
green card	la tarjeta verde	*lah tahrhehtah behrdeh*
greet	saludar	*sahloodahr*
grey (hair)	canoso	*kahnohsoh*
grey	gris	*grees*
grill (verb)	asar a la parrilla	*ahsahr ah lah pahrreelyah*
grilled	tostado	*tohstahdoh*
grocer's	la tienda de comestibles el almacén	*lah tyehndah deh kohmehsteeblehs ehl ahlmahcehn*
ground	la tierra	*lah tyehrrah*
group	el grupo	*ehl groopoh*
guest house	la pensión	*lah pehnsyohn*
guide (book)	la guía	*lah geeah*
guide (person)	el/la guía	*ehl/lah geeah*
guided tour	la visita guiada	*lah beeseetah geeahdah*
gynaecologist	el ginecólogo	*ehl heenehkohlohgoh*

H

hair	el pelo	*ehl pehloh*
hairbrush	el cepillo para el pelo	*ehl sehpeelyoh parah ehl pehloh*
hairdresser (ladies', men's)	la peluquería (de señoras, caballeros)	*lah pehlookehreeah (deh sehnyohrahs, kahbahlyehrohs)*
hairpins	las horquillas	*lahs ohrkeelyahs*
hairspray	la laca para el pelo	*lah lahkah pahrah ehl pehloh*
half	medio, media, la mitad	*mehdyoh, mehdyah, lah meetahdh*
half full	lleno hasta la mitad	*lyehnoh ahstah lah meetahdh*
half kilo	el medio kilo	*ehl mehdyoh keeloh*
hammer	el martillo	*ehl mahrteelyoh*
hand	la mano	*lah mahnoh*
hand brake	el freno de mano	*ehl frehnoh deh mahnoh*
handbag	el bolso de mano	*ehl bohlsoh deh mahnoh*
handkerchief	el pañuelo	*ehl pahnywehloh*
handmade	hecho a mano	*ehchoh ah mahnoh*
happy	contento	*kohntehntoh*
harbour	el puerto	*ehl pwehrtoh*

hard	duro	*dooroh*
haste	la prisa	*lah preesah*
hat	el sombrero	*ehl sohmbrehroh*
hay fever	la fiebre del heno	*lah fyehbreh dehl ehnoh*
hazelnut	la avellana	*lah ahbehlyahnah*
head	la cabeza	*lah kahbehsah*
headache	el dolor de cabeza	*ehl dohlohr deh kahbehsah*
health	la salud	*lah sahloodh*
health food shop	la tienda naturista	*lah tyehndah nahtooreestah*
hear	entender/oír	*ehntehndehr/oheer*
hearing aid	el audífono	*ehl ahoodeefohnoh*
heart	el corazón	*ehl kohrahsohn*
heart patient	el enfermo cardíaco	*ehl ehnfehrmoh kahrdeeahkoh*
heat	el calor	*ehl kahlohr*
heater	la calefacción	*lah kahlehfahksyohn*
heavy	pesado	*pehsahdoh*
heel	el talón	*ehl tahlohn*
heel (on shoe)	el tacón	*ehl tahkohn*
hello	hola	*ohlah*
helmet	el casco	*ehl kahskoh*
help (verb)	ayudar	*ahyoodahr*
help	la ayuda	*lah ahyoodah*
helping/portion	la ración	*lah rahsyohn*
herbal tea	la infusión	*lah eenfoosyohn*
here	aquí	*ahkee*
herring	el arenque	*ehl ahrehnkeh*
high	alto	*ahltoh*
high tide	la marea alta	*lah mahrehah ahltah*
highchair	la silla para niños	*lah seelyah pahrah neenyohs*
hiking	el excursionismo	*ehl ehxkoorsyohneesmoh*
hip	la cadera	*lah kahdehrah*
hire	alquilar	*ahlkeelahr*
hitchhike	hacer autostop	*ahsehr ahootohstohp*
hobby	el hobby	*ehl hohbee*
hold-up/robbery	el asalto	*ehl ahsahltoh*
holiday (public)	el día de fiesta	*ehl deeah deh fyehstah*
holiday house	el chalet	*ehl chahleh*
holiday park	la urbanización	*lah oorbahneesahsyohn*
holidays	las vacaciones	*lahs bahkahsyohnehs*
home (at)	en casa	*ehn kahsah*
homesickness	la nostalgia	*lah nohstahlhyah*
honest	sincero	*seensehroh*
honey	la miel	*lah myehl*
horizontal	horizontal	*ohreesohntahl*
horrible	horrible	*ohrreebleh*
horse	el caballo	*ehl kahbahlyoh*
hospital	el hospital	*ehl ohspeetahl*
hospitality	la hospitalidad	*lah ohspeetahleedahdh*
hot	cálido/caluroso	*kahleedoh/ kahloorohsoh*
hot (spicy)	picante	*peekahnteh*
hotel	el hotel	*ehl ohtehl*

hot-water bottle	la bolsa de agua caliente	*lah bohlsah deh ahgwah kahlyehnteh*
hour	la hora	*lah ohrah*
house	la casa	*lah kahsah*
household items	los artículos del hogar	*lohs ahrteekoolohs dehl ohgahr*
houses of parliament	la cámara de diputados	*lah kahmahrah deh deepootahdohs*
housewife	el ama de casa	*ehl ahmah deh kahsah*
how far?	¿a qué distancia?	*ah keh deestahnsyah?*
how long?	¿cuánto tiempo?	*kwahntoh tyehmpoh?*
how much?	¿cuánto?	*kwahntoh?*
how?	¿cómo?	*kohmoh?*
hunger	el hambre/el apetito	*ehl ahmbreh/ehl ahpehteetoh*
hurricane	el huracán	*ehl oorahkahn*
hurry	la prisa	*lah preesah*
husband	el marido	*ehl mahreedoh*
hut	el camarote	*ehl kahmahrohteh*
hyperventilation	la hiperventilación	*lah eepehr-behnteelahsyohn*

I

ice cream	el helado	*ehl ehlahdoh*
ice cubes	los cubitos de hielo	*lohs koobeetohs deh yehloh*
ice skating	el patinaje sobre hielo	*ehl pahteenahheh sohbreh yehloh*
idea	la idea	*lah eedehah*
identification card	el carnet de identidad	*ehl kahrneh deh eedehnteedahd*
identify	identificar	*eedehnteefeekahr*
ignition key	la llave de contacto	*lah lyahbeh deh kohntahktoh*
ill	enfermo	*ehnfehrmoh*
illness	la enfermedad	*lah ehnfehrmehdahd*
imagine	imaginarse	*eemahheenahrseh*
immediately	inmediatamente	*eenmehdyahtah-mehnteh*
import duty	los derechos de aduana	*lohs dehrehchohs deh ahdwahnah*
impossible	imposible	*eempohseebleh*
in	en	*ehn*
in the evening	por la tarde	*pohr lah tahrdeh*
in the morning	por la mañana	*pohr lah mahnyahnah*
included	incluido	*eenklooeedoh*
indicate	señalar	*sehnyahlahr*
indicator	el intermitente	*ehl eentehrmeetehnteh*
inexpensive	barato	*bahrahtoh*
infection (viral -, bacterial -)	la infección (vírica/viral, bacteriana)	*lah eenfehksyohn (beereekah, beerahl bahktehryahnah)*
inflammation	la inflamación	*lah eenflahmahsyohn*
information	la información	*lah eenfohrmahsyohn*
information office	la oficina de información	*lah ohfeeseenah deh eenfohrmahsyohn*
injection	la inyección	*lah eenyehksyohn*

injured	herido	*erhreedoh*
inner ear	el oído	*ehl oheedoh*
inner tube	la cámara	*lah kahmahrah*
innocent	inocente	*eenohsehnteh*
insect	el insecto	*ehl eensehktoh*
insect bite	la picadura de insecto	*lah peekahdoorah deh eensehktoh*
insect repellant	el aceite para los mosquitos	*ehl ahsehyteh pahrah lohs mohskeetohs*
inside	adentro	*ahdehntroh*
insole	la plantilla	*lah plahnteelyah*
instructions	las instrucciones	*lahs eenstrooksyohnehs*
insurance	el seguro	*ehl sehgooroh*
intermission	la pausa	*lah pahoosah*
international	internacional	*eentehrnahsyohnahl*
interpreter	el intérprete	*ehl eentehrprehteh*
intersection/crossing	el cruce	*ehl krooseh*
introduce oneself	presentarse	*prehsehntahrseh*
invite (verb)	invitar	*eenbeetahr*
iodine	el yodo	*ehl yohdoh*
iron (metal)	el hierro	*ehl yehrroh*
iron (verb)	planchar	*plahnchahr*
iron	la plancha	*lah plahnchah*
ironing board	la tabla de planchar	*lah tahblah deh plahnchahr*
island	la isla	*lah eeslah*
it's a pleasure	de nada	*deh nahdah*
Italian	italiano	*eetahlyahnoh*
itch	la picazón	*lah peekahsohn*

J

jack	el gato	*ehl gahtoh*
jacket	la chaqueta/el saco	*lah chahkehtah/ ehl sahkoh*
jam	la mermelada	*lah mehrmehlahdah*
January	enero	*ehnehroh*
jaw	la mandíbula	*lah mahndeeboolah*
jellyfish	la medusa	*lah mehdoosah*
jeweller	la joyería	*lah hoyehreeah*
jewels	las alhajas	*lahs ahlahhahs*
jog (verb)	hacer footing	*ahsehr footeen*
joke	la broma	*lah brohmah*
journey	el viaje	*ehl byahheh*
juice	el jugo	*ehl hoogoh*
July	julio	*hoolyoh*
jump leads	el cable de arranque	*ehl kahbleh deh ahrrahnkeh*
jumper	el jersey/pulóver	*ehl hehrsehee/ poolohbehr*
June	junio	*hoonyoh*

K

key	la llave	*lah lyahbeh*
kilo	el kilo	*ehl keeloh*
kilometre	kilómetro(s)	*keelohmehtroh(s)*
king	el rey	*ehl rehee*
kiss (verb)	besar	*behsahr*

kiss	el beso	*ehl behsoh*
kitchen	la cocina	*lah kohseenah*
knee	la rodilla	*lah rohdeelyah*
knee socks	las medias cortas	*lahs mehdyahs kohrtahs*
knife	el cuchillo	*ehl koocheelyoh*
know	saber	*sahbehr*

L

lace	el encaje	*ehl ehnkahheh*
ladies'	el baño para señoras	*ehl bahnyoh pahrah sehnyohrahs*
lake	el lago	*ehl lahgoh*
lamp	la lámpara	*lah lahmpahrah*
land (verb)	aterrizar	*ahtehrreesahr*
lane	el carril	*ehl kahrreel*
language	el idioma	*ehl eedyohmah*
large	grande	*grahndeh*
last	pasado, último	*pahsahdoh, oolteemoh*
last night	anoche	*ahnohcheh*
late	tarde	*tahrdeh*
later	luego	*lwehgoh*
latest (at the)	a más tardar	*ah mahs tahrdahr*
laugh	reír	*reheer*
launderette	la lavandería (automática)	*lah lahbahndehreeah (ahootohmahteekah)*
law	el derecho	*ehl dehrehchoh*
laxative	el laxante	*ehl lahxahnteh*
leak	la fuga, gotera	*lah foogah, gohtehrah*
leather	la piel, el cuero	*lah pyehl, ehl kwehroh*
leather goods	los artículos de piel	*lohs ahrteekoolohs deh pyehl*
leave (verb)	partir, salir	*pahrteer, sahleer*
leek	el puerro, porro	*ehl pwehrroh, pohroh*
left (on the)	a la izquierda	*ah lah eeskyehrdah*
left	izquierda	*eeskyehrdah*
left luggage	el depósito de equipajes	*ehl dehpohseetoh deh ehkeepahhehs*
leg	la pierna	*lah pyehrnah*
lemon	el limón	*ehl leemohn*
lemonade	la limonada	*lah leemohnahdah*
lend	prestar	*prehstahr*
lens	el objetivo	*ehl ohbhehteeboh*
lentils	las lentejas	*lahs lehntehhahs*
less	menos	*mehnohs*
lesson	la clase	*lah klahseh*
letter	la carta	*lah kahrtah*
lettuce	la lechuga	*lah lehchoogah*
level crossing	el paso a nivel	*ehl pahsoh ah neebehl*
library	la biblioteca	*lah beeblyohtehkah*
lie	mentir	*mehnteer*
lie down	estar tumbado	*ehstahr toombahdoh*
lift (hitchhike)	el viaje (en autostop)	*ehl byahheh (ehn ahootohstohp)*
lift (in building)	el ascensor/elevador	*ehl ahsehnsohr ehlehbahdohr*
lift (ski)	el telesquí, el telesilla	*ehl tehlehskee, ehl tehlehseelyah*

light (for cigarette)	el fuego	*ehl fwehgoh*
light (not dark)	claro	*klahroh*
light (not heavy)	ligero	*leehehroh*
lighter	el mechero encendedor	*ehl mehchehroh* *ehnsehndehdohr*
lighthouse	el faro	*ehl fahroh*
lightning	el rayo	*ehl rahyoh*
like	gustar	*goostahr*
line	la línea	*lah leenehah*
linen	el hilo, el lino	*ehl eeloh, ehl leenoh*
lipstick	el lápiz de labios	*ehl lahpees deh lahbyohs*
liqueur	el licor	*ehl leekohr*
liquorice	el regaliz	*ehl rehgahlees*
listen	escuchar	*ehskoochahr*
literature	la literatura	*lah leetehrahtoorah*
litre	el litro	*ehl leetroh*
little	poco	*pohkoh*
live (verb)	vivir	*beebeer*
live together	vivir con otra persona	*beebeer kohn ohtrah pehrsohnah*
lobster	la langosta	*lah lahngohstah*
local	local	*lohkahl*
lock	la cerradura	*lah sehrrahdoorah*
long	largo	*lahrgoh*
look (verb)	mirar	*meerahr*
look for	buscar	*booskahr*
look up (person)	buscar	*booskahr*
lorry	el camión	*ehl kahmyohn*
lose	perder	*pehrdehr*
loss	la pérdida	*lah pehrdeedah*
lost (to get)	perderse, extraviarse	*pehrdehrseh,* *ehxtrahbyahrseh*
lost	extraviado, perdido	*ehxtrahbyahdoh, pehrdeedoh*
lost item	extravío	*ehxtrahbeeoh*
lost property office	los objetos perdidos	*lohs ohbhehtohs pehrdeedohs*
lotion	la loción	*lah lohsyohn*
loud	alto	*ahltoh*
love (be in - with)	estar enamorado de	*ehstahr ehnahmohrahdoh deh*
love (verb)	querer	*kehrehr*
love	el amor	*ehl ahmohr*
low	bajo	*bahhoh*
low tide	la marea baja	*lah mahrehah bahhah*
luck	la suerte	*lah swehrteh*
luggage	el equipaje	*ehl ehkeepahheh*
luggage locker	la consigna automática	*lah kohnseegnah ahootohmahteekah*
lunch	el almuerzo, la comida	*ehl ahlmwehrsoh, lah kohmeedah*
lungs	los pulmones	*lohs poolmohnehs*

M

macaroni	los macarrones	*lohs mahkahrrohnehs*
madam/Mrs	señora	*sehnyohrah*
magazine	la revista	*lah rehbeestah*

magnificent	magnífico	*mahgneefeekoh*
mail	el correo	*ehl kohrrehoh*
main post office	la oficina central de Correos	*ah ohfeeseenah sehntrahl deh kohrrehohs*
main road	la carretera principal	*lah kahrrehtehrah preenseepahl*
make an appointment	pedir hora/cita	*pehdeer ohrah/seetah*
make love	acostarse/hacer el amor	*ahkohstahrseh/ahsehr ehl ahmohr*
makeshift	provisional(mente)	*prohbeesyohnahl (mehnteh)*
man	el hombre	*ehl ohmbreh*
manager	el encargado	*ehl ehnkahrgahdoh*
mandarin	la mandarina	*lah mahndahreenah*
manicure	la manicura	*lah mahneekoorah*
map	el mapa	*ehl mahpah*
marble	el mármol	*ehl mahrmohl*
March	marzo	*mahrsoh*
margarine	la margarina	*lah mahrgahreenah*
marina	el puerto deportivo	*ehl pwehrtoh dehpohrteeboh*
market	el mercado	*ehl mehrkahdoh*
marriage	el matrimonio	*ehl mahtreemohnyoh*
married	casado	*kahsahdoh*
mass	la misa	*lah meesah*
massage	el masaje	*ehl mahsahheh*
mat	mate	*mahteh*
matches	las cerillas	*lahs sehreelyahs*
	los fosforos	*lohs fohsfohrohs*
May	mayo	*mahyoh*
maybe	quizá	*keesah*
mayonnaise	la mayonesa	*lah mahyohnehsah*
mayor	el alcalde	*ehl ahlkahldeh*
meal	la comida	*lah kohmeedah*
mean (verb)	significar	*seegneefeekahr*
meat	la carne	*lah kahrneh*
medical insurance	el seguro de enfermedad	*ehl sehgooroh deh ehnfehrmehdahd*
medication	el medicamento	*ehl mehdeekahmehntoh*
medicine	el medicamento, la medicina	*ehl mehdeekahmehntoh, lah mehdeeseenah*
meet	conocer	*kohnohsehr*
melon	el melón	*ehl mehlohn*
membership	el ser socio	*ehl sehr sohsyoh*
menstruate	tener la regla	*tehnehr lah rehglah*
menstruation	la menstruación	*lah mehnstrooahsyohn*
menu	el menú, la carta	*ehl mehnoo, lah kahrtah*
menu of the day	el menú del día	*ehl mehnoo dehl deeah*
message	el recado/mensaje	*ehl rehkahdoh/ mehnsahheh*
metal	el metal	*ehl mehtahl*
meter (taxi)	el taxímetro	*ehl tahxeemehtroh*
metre	metro(s)	*mehtroh(s)*
migraine	la jaqueca	*lah hahkehkah*

mild (tobacco)	rubio	*roobyoh*
milk	la leche	*lah lehcheh*
millimetre(s)	milímetro(s)	*meeleemehtroh(s)*
milometer	el cuentakilómetros	*ehl kwehntah-keelohmehtrohs*
mince	la carne picada	*lah kahrneh peekahdah*
mineral water	el agua mineral	*ehl ahgwah meenehrahl*
minute	el minuto	*ehl meenootoh*
mirror	el espejo	*ehl ehspehoh*
miss (person)	echar de menos	*ehchahr deh mehnohs*
missing (be)	faltar	*fahltahr*
mistake	el error, la equivocación	*ehl ehrrohr, lah ehkeebohkahsyohn*
mistaken (be)	equivocarse	*ehkeebohkahrseh*
misunderstanding	el malentendido	*ehl mahlehntehndeedoh*
mixture	el jarabe, la poción	*ehl hahrahbeh, lah pohsyohn*
mocha	el moca	*ehl mohkah*
modern art	el arte moderno	*ehl ahrteh mohdehrnoh*
molar	la muela	*lah mwehlah*
moment	el momento	*ehl mohmehntoh*
Monday	el lunes	*ehl loonehs*
money	el dinero	*ehl deenehroh*
month	el mes	*ehl mehs*
moped	el ciclomotor	*ehl seeklohmohtohr*
morning-after pill	la píldora para el día después	*lah peeldohrah pahrah ehl deeah dehspwehs*
mosque	la mezquita	*lah mehskeetah*
motel	el motel	*ehl mohtehl*
mother	la madre	*lah mahdreh*
motor cross	el motocrós	*ehl mohtohkrohs*
motorbike	la moto	*lah mohtoh*
motorboat	la lancha motor	*lah lahnchah mohtohr*
motorway	la autovía, la autopista	*lah ahootohbeeah, lah ahootohpeestah*
mountain	la montaña	*lah mohntahnyah*
mountain hut	el refugio	*ehl rehfoohyoh*
mountaineering	el montañismo	*ehl mohntahnyeesmoh*
mountaineering shoes	las botas de alpinismo	*lahs bohtahs deh ahlpeeneesmoh*
mouse	el ratón	*ehl rahtohn*
mouth	la boca	*lah bohkah*
much/many	mucho	*moochoh*
multi-storey car park	el estacionamiento	*ehl ehstahsyohnah-myehntoh*
muscle	el músculo	*ehl mooskooloh*
muscle spasms	los calambres (en los músculos)	*lohs kahlahmbrehs (ehn lohs mooskoolohs)*
museum	el museo	*ehl moosehoh*
mushrooms	los champiñones	*lohs chahmpeenyohnehs*
music	la música	*lah mooseekah*
musical show	la comedia musical	*lah kohmehdyah mooseekahl*
mussels	los mejillones	*lohs meheelyohnehs*
mustard	la mostaza	*lah mohstahsah*

N

nail (on hand)	la uña	*lah oonyah*
nail	el clavo	*ehl klahboh*
nail polish	el esmalte (para uñas)	*ehl ehsmahlteh(pahrah oonyahs)*
nail polish remover	el quitaesmalte	*ehl keetahehsmahlteh*
nail scissors	las tijeras de uñas	*lahs teehehrahs pahrah oonyahs*
naked	desnudo	*dehsnoodoh*
nappy	el pañal	*ehl pahnyahl*
nationality	la nacionalidad	*lah nahsyohnahlee-dahdh*
nature	la naturaleza	*lah nahtoorahlehsah*
naturism	el naturismo	*ehl nahtooreesmoh*
nauseous	con náuseas	*kohn nahoosehahs*
near	junto a	*hoontoh ah*
nearby	cerca	*sehrkah*
necessary	necesario	*nehsehsahryoh*
neck	la nuca/el cuello	*lah nookah/ehl kwehlyoh*
necklace	la cadena/el collar	*lah kahdehnah/ ehl kohlyar*
needle	la aguja	*lah ahoohah*
negative	el negativo	*ehl nehgahteeboh*
neighbours	los vecinos	*lohs behseenohs*
nephew	el sobrino	*ehl sohbreenoh*
Netherlands	los Países Bajos	*lohs paheesehs bahhohs*
never	jamás/nunca	*hahmahs/noonkah*
new	nuevo	*nwehboh*
news	las noticias	*lahs nohteesyahs*
news stand	el quiosco	*ehl kyohskoh*
newspaper	el periódico	*ehl pehryohdeekoh*
next	próximo, que viene	*prohxeemoh, keh byehneh*
next to	al lado de	*ahl lahdoh deh*
nice (friendly)	amable	*ahmahbleh*
nice (to look at)	bonito, lindo	*bohneetoh, leendoh*
nice	bien, agradable	*byehn, ahgrahdahbleh*
niece	la sobrina	*lah sohbreenah*
night (at)	por la noche	*pohr lah nohcheh*
night	la noche	*lah nohcheh*
night duty	la guardia nocturna	*lah gwahrdyah nohktoornah*
nightclub	el cabaré	*ehl kahbahreh*
nightlife	la vida nocturna	*lah beedah nohktoornah*
nipple	la tetina/el chupón	*lah tehteenah/ ehl choopohn*
no	no	*noh*
no overtaking	la prohibición de adelantar	*lah proheebeesyohn deh ahdehlahntahr*
noise	el ruido	*ehl rooeedoh*
nonstop	sin escalas	*seen ehskahlahs*
no-one	nadie	*nahdyeh*
normal	normal, corriente	*nohrmahl, kohrryehnteh*
north	el norte	*ehl nohrteh*
nose	la nariz	*lah nahrees*

nose bleed	la hemorragia nasal	*lah ehmohrrahhyah nahsahl*
nose drops	las gotas para la nariz	*lahs gohtahs pahrah lah nahrees*
notepaper	el papel de escribir	*ehl pahpehl deh ehskreebeer*
nothing	nada	*nahdah*
November	noviembre	*nohbyehmbreh*
nowhere	en ninguna parte	*ehn neengoonah pahrteh*
nudist beach	la playa nudista	*lah plahyah noodeestah*
number	el número	*ehl noomehroh*
number plate	la matrícula	*lah mahtreekoolah*
nurse	la enfermera	*lah ehnfehrmehrah*
nutmeg	la nuez moscada	*lah nwehs mohskahdah*
nuts	los frutos secos/ las nueces	*lohs frootohs sehkohs/ lahs nwehsehs*

O

October	octubre	*ohktoobreh*
of course	claro	*klahroh*
off	podrido	*pohdreedoh*
offer	ofrecer	*ohfrehsehr*
office	la oficina	*lah ohfeeseenah*
off-licence	la bodega, la tienda de vinos y licores	*lah bohdehgah, lah tyehndah deh beenohs ee leekohrehs*
oil	el aceite	*ehl ahseyteh*
oil level	el nivel del aceite	*ehl neebehl deh ahseyteh*
ointment	la pomada, el ungüento	*lah pohmahdah, ehl oongwehntoh*
ointment for burns	la pomada contra las quemaduras	*lah pohmahdah kohntrah lahs kehmahdoorahs*
okay	de acuerdo	*deh ahkwehrdoh*
old	viejo	*byehhoh*
old part of town	el casco antiguo	*ehl kahskoh ahnteegwoh*
olive oil	el aceite de oliva	*ehl ahseyteh deh ohleebah*
olives	las aceitunas	*lahs ahseytoonahs*
omelette	la tortilla	*lah tohrteelyah*
on	sobre	*sohbreh*
on board	a bordo	*ah bohrdoh*
oncoming car	el vehículo que viene	*ehl beheekooloh keh byehneh*
one hundred grams	los cien gramos	*lohs syehn grahmohs*
one-way traffic	la dirección única	*lah deerehksyohn ooneekah*
onion	la cebolla	*lah sehbohlyah*
open (adj.)	abierto	*ahbyehrtoh*
open (verb)	abrir	*ahbreer*
opera	la ópera	*lah ohpehrah*
operate	operar	*ohpehrahr*
operator (telephone)	la operadora	*lah ohpehrahdohrah*

operetta	la opereta, la zarzuela	*lah ohpehrehtah, lah sahrswehlah*
opposite	al frente, enfrente de	*ahl frehnteh, ehnfrehnteh deh*
optician	la óptica	*lah ohpteekah*
orange	la naranja	*lah nahrahnhah*
orange (adj.)	naranja	*nahrahnhah*
orange juice	el jugo de naranja	*ehl hoogoh deh nahrahnhah*
order (in -,) tidy	en orden, ordenado	*ehn ohrdehn, ohrdehnahdo*
order (verb)	pedir	*pehdeer*
order	el pedido	*ehl pehdeedoh*
other	otro	*ohtroh*
other side	el otro lado	*ehl ohtroh lahdoh*
outside	afuera	*ahfwehrah*
overtake	adelantar/rebasar	*ahdehlahntahr/ rehbahsahr*
oysters	las ostras	*lahs ohstrahs*

P

page	la página	*lah pahheenah*
pain	el dolor	*ehl dohlohr*
painkiller	el analgésico	*ehl ahnahlhehseekoh*
paint (verb)	pintar	*peentahr*
paint	la pintura	*lah peentoorah*
painting (art)	el cuadro	*ehl kwahdroh*
painting (object)	la pintura	*lah peentoorah*
palace	el palacio	*ehl pahlahsyoh*
pancake	la crepe/ el panqueque	*lah krehp/ ehl pahnkehkeh*
pane	el cristal	*ehl kreestahl*
pants (briefs)	las bragas	*lahs brahgahs*
panty liner	el protegeslip	*ehl prohtehhehsleep*
paper	el papel	*ehl pahpehl*
paraffin oil	el querosén	*ehl kehrohsehn*
parasol	el quitasol	*ehl keetahsohl*
parcel	el paquete	*ehl pahkehteh*
pardon	perdone	*pehrdohneh*
parents	los padres	*lohs pahdrehs*
park	el parque	*ehl pahrkeh*
park (verb)	estacionarse	*ehstahsyohnahrseh*
parking space	el lugar para estacionar	*ehl loogahr pahrah ehstahsyohnahr*
parsley	el perejil	*ehl pehrehheel*
partition	la secreción	*lah sehkrehsyohn*
partner	la pareja	*lah pahrehhah*
party	la fiesta	*lah fyehstah*
passable	practicable	*prahkteekahbleh*
passenger	el pasajero	*ehl pahsahhehroh*
passport	el pasaporte	*ehl pahsahpohrteh*
passport photo	la foto de carnet	*lah fohtoh deh kahrneh*
patient	el paciente	*ehl pahsyehnteh*
pavement	la acera/la banqueta	*lah ahsehrah/ lah bahnkehtah*
pay (verb)	pagar	*pahgahr*
pay the bill	pagar la cuenta	*pahgahr lah kwehntah*

peach	el durazno	*ehl doorahsnoh*
peanuts	los cacahuetes maníes	*lohs kahkahwehtehs mahnyes*
pear	la pera	*lah pehrah*
peas	los chícharos las arvejas	*lohs cheechahrohs lahs ahrbehhas*
pedal	el pedal	*ehl pehdahl*
pedestrian crossing	el paso de peatones	*ehl pahsoh deh pehahtohnehs*
pedicure	la pedicura	*lah pehdeekoorah*
pen	la pluma	*lah ploomah*
pencil (hard/soft)	el lápiz (duro/blando)	*ehl lahpees (dooroh /blahndoh)*
penis	el pene	*ehl pehneh*
pepper (capsicum)	el pimiento/chile	*ehl peemyehntoh cheeleh*
pepper (condiment)	la pimienta	*lah peemyehntah*
performance	la función de teatro /música	*lah foonsyohn deh tehahtroh/mooseekah*
perfume	el perfume	*ehl pehrfoomeh*
perm (verb)	hacer una permanente	*ahsehr oonah pehrmahnehnteh*
perm	la permanente	*lah pehrmahnehnteh*
permit	el permiso	*ehl pehrmeesoh*
person	la persona	*lah pehrsohnah*
personal	personal	*pehrsohnahl*
petrol	la gasolina/ bencina/nafta	*lah gahsohleenah/ behnseenah/naftah*
petrol station	la gasolinera/ estación de servicio	*lah gahsohleenehrah ehstahsyohn deh sehrbeesyoh*
pets	los animales domésticos	*lohs ahneemahles dohmehsteekohs*
pharmacy	la farmacia	*lah fahrmahsyah*
phone (by)	por teléfono	*pohr tehlehfohnoh*
phone (tele-)	el teléfono	*ehl tehlehfohnoh*
phone (verb)	llamar por teléfono	*lyahmahr pohr tehlehfohnoh*
phone box	la caseta/cabina telefónica	*lah kahsehtah/ kahbeenah tehlehfohneekah*
phone directory	la guía de teléfonos	*lah geeah deh tehlehfohnohs*
phone number	el número de teléfono	*ehl noomehroh deh tehlehfohnoh*
photo	la foto	*lah fohtoh*
photocopier	la fotocopiadora	*lah fohtohkohpyahdohrah*
photocopy (verb)	fotocopiar	*fohtohkohpyahr*
photocopy	la fotocopia	*lah fohtohkohpyah*
pick up (fetch person)	(ir a) buscar, pasar a buscar	*(eer ah) booskahr, pahsahr ah booskahr*
picnic	el picnic	*ehl peekneek*
piece of clothing	la prenda	*lah prehndah*
pier	el muelle	*ehl mwehlyeh*
pigeon	la paloma	*lah pahlohmah*
pill (contraceptive)	la píldora (anticonceptiva)	*lah peeldohrah (ahnteekohnsehpteebah)*

pillow	la almohada	*lah ahlmohahdah*
pillowcase	la funda de almohada	*lah foondah deh ahlmohahdah*
pin	el alfiler	*ehl ahlfeelehr*
pineapple	la piña	*lah peenyah*
pipe	la pipa	*lah peepah*
pipe tobacco	el tabaco de pipa	*ehl tahbahkoh deh peepah*
pity	lástima	*lahsteemah*
place of entertainment	el sitio para salir	*ehl seetyoh pahrah sahleer*
place of interest	el punto de interés	*ehl poontoh deh eentehrehs*
plan/map	el plano	*ehl plahnoh*
plant	la planta	*lah plahntah*
plasters	las tiritas, los esparadrapos	*lahs teereetahs, lohs ehspahrah-drahpohs*
plastic	el plástico	*ehl plahsteekoh*
plastic bag	la bolsita	*lah bohlseetah*
plate	el plato	*ehl plahtoh*
platform	la vía, el andén	*lah beeah, ehl ahndehn*
play (theatre)	la obra de teatro	*lah ohbrah deh tehahtroh*
play (verb)	jugar	*hoogahr*
playground	el parque infantil	*ehl pahrkeh eenfahnteel*
playing cards	los naipes	*lohs naheepehs*
pleasant	agradable	*ahgrahdahbleh*
please	por favor	*pohr fahbohr*
pleasure	el placer	*ehl plahsehr*
plum	la ciruela	*lah seerwehlah*
pocketknife	la navaja	*lah nahbahhah*
point (verb)	indicar	*eendeekahr*
poison	el veneno	*ehl behnehnoh*
police	la policía	*lah pohleeseeah*
police station	la comisaría	*la kohmeesahreeah*
policeman	el guardia	*ehl gwahrdyah*
pond	el estanque	*ehl ehstahnkeh*
pony	el poney	*ehl pohnehy*
pop concert	el concierto pop	*ehl kohnsyehrtoh pohp*
population	la población	*lah pohblahsyohn*
pork	la carne de cerdo/puerco/chanco	*lah kahrneh deh sehrdoh/pwehrkoh/chahnchoh*
port wine	el oporto	*ehl ohpohrtoh*
porter	el portero	*ehl pohrtehroh*
post code	el código postal	*ehl cohdeegoh pohstahl*
post office	la oficina de Correos	*lah ohfeeseenah deh cohrrehohs*
postage	el franqueo	*ehl frahnkehoh*
postbox	el buzón	*ehl boosohn*
postcard	la (tarjeta) postal	*lah (tahrhehtah) pohstahl*
postman	el cartero	*ehl kahrtehroh*
potato	la patata/papa	*lah pahtahtah/pahpah*

poultry	las aves	*lahs ahbehs*
powdered milk	la leche en polvo	*lah lehcheh ehn pohlboh*
power point	la toma de corriente	*lah tohmah deh kohrryehnteh*
pram	el cochecito	*ehl kohchehseetoh*
prawns	las gambas los camarones	*lahs gahmbahs* *lohs kahmahrohnehs*
precious	querido	*kehreedoh*
prefer	preferir	*prehfehreer*
preference	la preferencia	*lah prehfehrehnsyah*
pregnant	embarazada	*ehmbahrahsahdah*
present	presente	*prehsehnteh*
present (gift)	el regalo	*ehl rehgahloh*
press (verb)	apretar	*ahprehtahr*
pressure	la tensión/ la presión	*lah tehnsyohn/* *lah prehsyohn*
price	el precio	*ehl prehsyoh*
price list	la lista de precios	*lah leestah deh prehsyohs*
print (verb)	copiar	*kohpyahr*
print	la copia	*lah kohpyah*
probably	probablemente	*prohbahblehmehnteh*
problem	el problema	*ehl prohblehmah*
profession	la profesión	*lah prohfehsyohn*
programme	el programa	*ehl prohgrahmah*
pronounce	pronunciar	*prohnoonsyahr*
propane camping gas	el gas propano	*ehl gahs prohpahnoh*
pull	sacar/jalar	*sahkahr/halahr*
pull a muscle	distender un músculo	*deestehndehr oon mooskooloh*
pure	puro	*pooroh*
purple	violeta	*beeohlehtah*
purse	el monedero	*ehl mohnehdehroh*
push	empujar	*ehmpoohahr*
puzzle	el rompecabezas	*ehl rohmpehkahbehsahs*
pyjamas	el pijama	*ehl peehahmah*

Q

quarter	la cuarta parte	*lah kwahrtah pahrteh*
quarter of an hour	el cuarto de hora	*ehl kwahrtoh deh ohrah*
queen	la reina	*lah reheenah*
question	la pregunta	*lah prehgoontah*
quick	rápido	*rahpeedoh*
quiet	tranquilo	*trahnkeeloh*

R

radio	la radio	*lah rahdyoh*
railways	los ferrocarriles	*lohs fehrrohkahrreelehs*
rain (verb)	llover	*lyohbehr*
rain	la lluvia	*lah lyoobyah*
raincoat	el impermeable	*ehl eempehrmehahbleh*
raisins	las uvas pasas	*lahs oobahs pahsahs*
rape	la violación	*lah beeohlahsyohn*
rapids	el rápido	*ehl rahpeedoh*
rash (skin)	la erupción cutánea	*lah ehroopsyohn kootahnehah*

raspberries	las frambuesas	*lahs frahmbwehsahs*
raw	crudo	*kroodoh*
raw ham	el jamón crudo (serrano)	*ehl hahmohn kroodoh sehrrahnoh*
raw vegetables	las verduras crudas	*lahs behrdoorahs kroodahs*
razor blades	las hojas de afeitar	*lahs ohahs deh ahfeheetahr*
read (verb)	leer	*lehehr*
ready	listo	*leestoh*
really	en realidad	*ehn rehahleedahdh*
receipt	el recibo	*ehl rehseeboh*
recipe	la receta	*lah rehsehtah*
reclining chair	la reposera	*lah rehpohsehrah*
recommend	recomendar	*rehkohmehndahr*
rectangle	el rectángulo	*ehl rehktahngooloh*
red	rojo	*rohhoh*
red wine	el vino tinto	*ehl beenoh teentoh*
refrigerator	el refrigerador	*ehl rehfreehehrahdohr*
regards	recuerdos	*rehkwehrdohs*
region	la región	*lah rehhyohn*
registered	certificado	*sehrteefeekahdoh*
relatives	los parientes	*lohs pahryehntehs*
reliable	fiable/seguro	*fyahbleh/sehgooroh*
religion	la religión	*lah rehleehyohn*
rent out	alquilar	*ahlkeelahr*
repair (verb)	arreglar	*ahrrehglahr*
repairs	el arreglo	*ehl ahrrehgloh*
repeat	repetir	*rehpehteer*
report	el atestado	*ehl ahtehstahdoh*
	la declaración	*lah dehklahrahsyohn*
resent	tomar a mal	*tohmahr ah mahl*
responsible	responsable	*rehspohnsahbleh*
rest (verb)	descansar	*dehskahnsahr*
restaurant	el restaurante	*ehl rehstahoorahnteh*
retired	jubilado	*hoobeeladoh*
retirement	la jubilación	*lah hoobeelahsyohn*
return (ticket)	el boleto de ida y vuelta	*ehl bohlehtoh deh eedah ee bwehltah*
reverse (vehicle)	dar marcha atrás	*dahr mahrchah ahtrahs*
rheumatism	el reuma	*ehl rehoomah*
rice	el arroz	*ehl ahrrohs*
ridiculous	tontería(s)	*tohntehreeah(s)*
riding (horseback)	montar a caballo	*mohntahr ah kahbahlyoh*
riding school	el picadero	*ehl peekahdehroh*
right	derecha	*dehrehchah*
right (on the)	a la derecha	*ah lah dehrehchah*
right of way	la preferencia	*lah prehfehrehnsyah*
ripe	maduro	*mahdooroh*
risk	el riesgo	*ehl ryehsgoh*
river	el río	*ehl reeoh*
road	el camino	*ehl kahmeenoh*
roadway	la calzada	*lah kahlsahdah*
roasted	asado	*ahsahdoh*
rock	la roca	*lah rohkah*
rolling tobacco	el tabaco para liar	*ehl tahbahkoh pahrah leeahr*

roof rack	la baca	*lah bahkah*
room	la habitación	*lah ahbeetahsyohn*
room number	el número de la habitación	*ehl noomehroh deh lah ahbeetahsyohn*
room service	el servicio en la habitación	*ehl sehrbeesyoh ehn lah ahbeetahsyohn*
rope	la cuerda	*lah kwehrdah*
rosé	el vino rosado	*ehl beenoh rohsahdoh*
roundabout	la rotonda	*lah rohtohndah*
route	la ruta	*lah rootah*
rowing boat	el bote de remos	*ehl bohteh deh rehmohs*
rubber	la goma	*lah gohmah*
rubbish	tontería(s)	*tohntehreeah(s)*
rucksack	la mochila	*lah mohcheelah*
rude	descortés/ maleducado	*dehskohrtehs/ mahlehdookahdoh*
ruins	las ruinas	*lahs rweenahs*
run into	encontrar	*ehnkohntrahr*

S

sad	triste	*treesteh*
safari	el safari	*ehl sahfahree*
safe	la caja fuerte	*lah kahhah fwehrteh*
safe/secure	seguro	*sehgooroh*
safety pin	el imperdible/ alfiler de seguridad	*ehl eempehrdeebleh/ ahlfeelehr deh sehgooreedad*
sail	la vela	*lah behlah*
sailing boat	el velero	*ehl behlehroh*
salad	la ensalada	*lah ehnsahlahdah*
salad oil	el aceite	*ehl ahsehyteh*
salami	el salame	*ehl sahlahmeh*
sale	las rebajas, la liquidación	*lahs rehbahhahs, lah leekeedahsyohn*
salt	la sal	*lah sahl*
same	mismo	*meesmoh*
same	lo mismo	*loh meesmoh*
sandwich	el sandwich	*ehl sandwich*
sandy beach	la playa de arena	*lah plahyah deh ahrehnah*
sanitary towel	la compresa/ toalla sanitaria	*lah kohmprehsah/tohah-lyah sahneetahreeah*
sardines	las sardinas	*lahs sahrdeenahs*
satisfied	contento	*kohntehntoh*
Saturday	el sábado	*ehl sahbahdoh*
sauce	la salsa	*lah sahlsah*
saucepan	la cacerola	*lah kahsehrohlah*
sauna	la sauna	*lah sahoonah*
sausage	el embutido/ la salchicha	*ehl ehmbooteedoh/ lah sahlcheechah*
savoury	salado	*sahlahdoh*
say (verb)	decir	*dehseer*
scarf	la bufanda (woollen)	*lah boofahndah*
scarf	el pañuelo	*ehl pahnywehloh*
scenic walk	la visita a la ciudad (a pie)	*lah beeseetah ah lah syoodahdh (ah pyeh)*

school	la escuela	*lah ehskwehlah*
scissors	las tijeras	*lahs teehehrahs*
scooter	la vespa	*lah behspah*
scorpion	el escorpión	*ehl ehskohrpyohn*
scrambled eggs	los huevos revueltos	*lohs wehbohs rehbwehltohs*
screw	el tornillo	*ehl tohrneelyoh*
screwdriver	el destornillador	*ehl dehstohrneelyahdohr*
sculpture	la escultura	*lah ehskooltoorah*
sea	el mar	*ehl mahr*
seasick	mareado	*mahrehahdoh*
seat	el asiento, la butaca	*ehl ahsyehntoh, lah bootahkah*
second (adj.)	segundo	*sehgoondoh*
second	el segundo	*ehl sehgoondoh*
second-hand	de segunda mano	*deh sehgoondah mahnoh*
sedative	el calmante	*ehl kahlmahnteh*
see (person)	visitar	*beeseetahr*
see	mirar	*meerahr*
self-timer	el disparador automático	*ehl deespahrahdohr ahootohmahteekoh*
semi-skimmed	semidesnatado semidescremado	*sehmeedehsnahtahdoh sehmeedehskrehmahdoh*
send	enviar	*ehnbyahr*
sentence	la frase	*lah frahseh*
September	septiembre	*sehptyehmbreh*
serious	grave	*grahbeh*
service	el servicio	*ehl sehrbeesyoh*
serviette	la servilleta	*lah sehrbeelyehtah*
set (verb)	marcar	*mahrkahr*
sewing thread	el hilo de coser	*ehl eeloh deh kohsehr*
shade	la sombra	*lah sohmbrah*
shallow	poco profundo	*pohkoh prohfoondoh*
shampoo	el champú	*ehl chahmpoo*
shark	el tiburón	*ehl teeboorohn*
shave (verb)	afeitar	*ahfeheetahr*
shaver	la afeitadora eléctrica	*lah ahfehytahdohrah ehlehktreekah*
shaving brush	la brocha de afeitar	*lah brohchah deh ahfeheetahr*
shaving cream	la crema de afeitar	*lah krehmah deh ahfeheetahr*
shaving soap	el jabón de afeitar	*ehl hahbohn deh ahfeheetahr*
sheet	la sábana	*lah sahbahnah*
sherry	el jerez	*ehl hehrehth*
shirt	la camisa	*lah kahmeesah*
shoe	el zapato	*ehl thahpahtoh*
shoe polish	la crema de zapatos	*lah krehmah deh sahpahtohs*
shoe shop	la zapatería	*lah sahpahtehreeah*
shoelaces	los cordones/ las agujetas	*lohs kohrdohnehs/ lahs ahgoohehtahs*
shoemaker	el zapatero	*ehl sahpahtehroh*
shop (verb)	hacer la compra	*ahsehr lah kohmprah*

shop	la tienda	*lah tyehndah*
shop assistant	la vendedora	*lah behndehdohrah*
shop window	el escaparate	*ehl ehskahpahrahteh*
shopping centre	el centro comercial	*ehl sehntroh kohmehrsyahl*
short	corto	*kohrtoh*
short circuit	el cortocircuito	*ehl kohrtohseer-kweetoh*
shoulder	el hombro	*ehl ohmbroh*
show	el espectáculo	*ehl ehspehktahkooloh*
shower	la ducha	*lah doochah*
shutter	el obturador	*ehl ohbtoorahdohr*
sieve	el tamiz/la coladera	*ehl tahmees/ lah kohlahdehrah*
sign (verb)	firmar	*feermahr*
sign	el cartel	*ehl kahrtehl*
signature	la firma	*lah feermah*
signposted walk	la excursión señalizada	*lah ehxkooresyohn sehnyahleesahdah*
silence	el silencio	*ehl seelehnsyoh*
silver	la plata	*lah plahtah*
silver-plated	plateado	*plahtehahdoh*
simple	sencillo	*sehnseelyoh*
single (unmarried)	soltero	*sohltehroh*
single	individual	*eendeebeedwahl*
single ticket	el boleto de ida	*ehl bohlehtoh deh eedah*
sir	señor	*sehnyohr*
sister	la hermana	*lah ehrmahnah*
sit	estar sentado	*ehstahr sehntahdoh*
size (shoes)	el número	*ehl noomehroh*
size	la talla	*lah tahlyah*
ski boots	las botas de esquí	*lahs bohtahs deh ehskee*
ski goggles	las gafas de esquí	*lahs gahfahs deh ehskee*
ski instructor	el profesor de esquí	*ehl prohfehsohr deh ehskee*
ski lessons/class	la clase de esquiar	*lah klahseh deh ehskeeahr*
ski lift	el telesquí	*ehl tehlehskee*
ski pants	los pantalones de esquiar	*lohs pahntahlohnehs deh ehskeeahr*
ski pass	el bono (de remontes/esquí)	*ehl bohnoh (deh rehmohntehs/ehskee)*
ski slope	la pista de esquí (alpino)	*lah peestah deh ehskee (ahlpeenoh)*
ski stick	el bastón de esquí	*ehl bahstohn deh ehskee*
ski suit	el traje de esquiar	*ehl trahheh deh ehskeeahr*
ski wax	la cera para esquí	*lah sehrah pahrah ehskee*
ski/skiing	esquiar, el esquí	*ehskeeahr, ehl ehskee*
skin	la piel	*lah pyehl*
skirt	la falda	*lah fahldah*
skis	los esquís	*lohs ehskees*
sleep (verb)	dormir	*dohrmeer*
sleep well!	que descanse	*keh dehskahnseh*
sleeping car	el coche cama	*ehl kohcheh kahmah*

sleeping pills	los somníferos	*lohs sohmneefehrohs*
slide	la diapositiva	*lah deeahpohseeteebah*
slip (women's)	la combinación	*lah kohmbeenahsyohn*
slip road	la entrada	*lah ehntrahdah*
slow	despacio	*dehspahsyoh*
slow train	el tren local/autovía	*ehl trehn lohkahl ahootohbeeah*
small	pequeño	*pehkehnyoh*
small change	el cambio, el dinero suelto	*ehl kahmbyoh, ehl deenehroh swehltoh*
smell unpleasant (verb)	oler mal	*ohlehr mahl*
smoke	el humo	*ehl oomoh*
smoke (verb)	fumar	*foomahr*
smoked	ahumado	*ahoomahdoh*
smoking compartment	el departamento de fumadores	*ehl dehpahrtahmehntoh deh foomahdohrehs*
snake	la serpiente	*lah sehrpyehnteh*
snorkel	el esnórquel	*ehl ehsnohrkehl*
snow (verb)	nevar	*nehbahr*
snow	la nieve	*lah nyehbeh*
snow chains	la cadena antideslizante	*lah kahdehnah ahnteedehsleesahnte*
soap	el jabón	*ehl hahbohn*
soap box	la jabonera	*lah hahbohnehrah*
soap powder	el jabón en polvo	*ehl hahbohn ehn pohlboh*
soccer	el fútbol	*ehl footbohl*
soccer match	el partido de fútbol	*ehl pahrteedoh deh footbohl*
socket	el enchufe	*ehl ehnchoofeh*
socks	los calcetines	*lohs kahlsehteenehs*
soft drink	el refresco	*ehl rehfrehskoh*
sole (fish)	el lenguado	*ehl lehngwahdoh*
sole	la suela	*lah swehlah*
solicitor	el abogado	*ehl ahbohgahdoh*
someone	alguien	*ahlguyehn*
sometimes	a veces	*ah behsehs*
somewhere	en alguna parte	*ehn ahlgoonah pahrteh*
son	el hijo	*ehl eehoh*
soon	pronto	*prohntoh*
sorbet	el sorbete	*ehl sohrbehteh*
sore	la úlcera	*lah oolsehrah*
sore throat	el dolor de garganta	*ehl dohlohr deh gahrgahntah*
sorry	perdón	*pehrdohn*
sort/type	la clase	*lah klahseh*
soup	la sopa	*lah sohpah*
sour	agrio	*ahgreeoh*
sour cream	la nata/crema ácida	*lah nahtah/krehmah ahseedah*
source	la fuente	*lah fwehnteh*
south	el sur	*ehl soor*
souvenir	el recuerdo de viaje	*ehl rehkwehrdoh deh byahheh*
spaghetti	los espaguetis	*lohs ehspahghehtees*
Spanish	español	*ehspahnyohl*
spanner (openended)	la llave (de boca)	*lah lyahbeh (deh bohkah)*

spanner	la llave de tuercas	*lah lyahbeh deh twehrkahs*
spare	la reserva	*lah rehsehrbah*
spare part	la pieza de recambio	*lah pyehsah deh rehkahmbyoh*
spare tyre	el neumático de reserva	*ehl nehoomahteekoh deh rehsehrbah*
spare wheel	la rueda de auxilio	*lah rwehdah deh ahookseeleeoh*
speak	hablar	*ahblahr*
special	especial	*ehspehsyahl*
specialist	el especialista	*ehl ehspesyahleestah*
specialty	la especialidad	*lah ehspehsyahleedahd*
speed limit	la velocidad máxima	*lah behlohseedahd mahxeemah*
spell (verb)	deletrear	*dehlehtrehahr*
spicy	picante	*peekahnteh*
splinter	la astilla	*lah ahsteelyah*
spoon	la cuchara	*lah koochahrah*
spoonful	la cucharada	*lah koochahrahdah*
sport (play)	hacer deporte	*ahsehr dehpohrteh*
sport	el deporte	*ehl dehpohrteh*
sports centre	la sala de deportes	*lah sahlah deh dehpohrtehs*
spot/place	el sitio	*ehl seetyoh*
sprain (verb)	torcerse	*tohrsehrseh*
spring	la primavera	*lah preemahbehrah*
square	el cuadrado	*ehl kwahdrahdoh*
square (town)	la plaza/el zócalo	*lah plahsah/ehl sohkahloh*
square metre(s)	metro(s) cuadrado(s)	*mehtroh(s) kwahdrahdoh(s)*
squash	el squash	*ehl skwahsh*
stadium	el estadio	*ehl ehstahdyoh*
stain	la mancha	*lah mahnchah*
stain remover	el quitamanchas	*ehl keetahmahnchahs*
stairs	las escaleras	*lahs ehskahlehrahs*
stalls (theatre)	la platea	*lah plahtehah*
stamp	la estampilla/ el timbre	*lah ehstahmpeelyah/ ehl teembreh*
start (car)	arrancar	*ahrrahnkahr*
station	la estación	*lah ehstahsyohn*
statue	la estatua	*lah ehstahtooah*
stay (lodge)	alojarse	*ahlohhahrseh*
stay (verb)	quedarse	*kehdahrseh*
stay	la estancia	*lah ehstahnsyah*
steal (verb)	robar	*rohbahr*
steel, stainless	el acero, inoxidable	*ehl ahsehroh, eenohxeedahbleh*
stench	el mal olor	*ehl mahl ohlohr*
sting (verb)	picar	*peekahr*
stitch (med.)	el punto	*ehl poontoh*
stitch (verb)	suturar	*sootoorahr*
stock	el caldo	*ehl kahldoh*
stockings	las medias	*lahs mehdyahs*
stomach	el estómago, el vientre	*ehl ehstohmahgoh, ehl byehntreh*

stomach ache	el dolor de vientre/ estómago	ehl dohlohr deh byehntreh/ ehstohmahgoh
stomach cramps	los retortijones	lohs rehtohrteehohnehs
stools	las heces	lahs ehsehs
stop (verb)	parar	pahrahr
stop	la parada	lah pahrahdah
stopover	la escala	lah ehskahlah
storm	la tormenta	lah tohrmehntah
straight	liso	leesoh
straight ahead	derecho	dehrehchoh
straw	la pajita/el popote	lah pahheetah/ ehl pohpohteh
strawberries	las fresas/frutillas	lahs frehsahs/ frooteelyahs
street	la calle	lah kahlyeh
street side	el lado de la calle	ehl lahdoh deh lah kahlyeh
strike	la huelga	lah wehlgah
strong (tobacco)	negro	nehgroh
study (verb)	estudiar	ehstoodyahr
stuffing	el relleno	ehl rehlyehnoh
subscriber's number	el número de abonado	ehl noomehroh deh ahbohnahdoh
subtitled	subtitulada	soobteetoolahdah
succeed	salir bien	sahleer byehn
sugar	el azúcar	ehl ahsookahr
sugar lumps	los terrones de azúcar	lohs tehrrohnehs deh ahsookahr
suit	el traje	ehl trahheh
suitcase	la maleta/valija	lah mahlehtah/ bahleehah
summer	el verano	ehl behrahnoh
summertime	la hora de verano	lah ohrah deh behrahnoh
sun	el sol	ehl sohl
sun hat	el sombrero de playa	ehl sohmbrehroh deh plahyah
sunbathe	tomar el sol	tohmahr ehl sohl
Sunday	el domingo	ehl dohmeengoh
sunglasses	las gafas/los lentes de sol	lahs gahfahs/lohs lehntehs de sohl
sunrise	la salida del sol	lah sahleedah dehl sohl
sunset	la puesta del sol	lah pwehstah dehl sohl
sunstroke	la insolación	lah eensohlahthyohn
suntan lotion	la crema solar	lah krehmah sohlahr
suntan oil	el aceite bronceador	ehl ahsehyteh brohnthehahdohr
supermarket	el supermercado	ehl soopehrmehrkahdoh
surcharge	el suplemento	ehl sooplehmehntoh
surf	el surf	ehl soorf
surf board	la tabla de surf	lah tahblah deh soorf
surgery	el consultorio	ehl kohnsooltohryoh
surname	el apellido	ehl ahpehlyeedoh
surprise	la sorpresa	lah sohrprehsah
swallow (verb)	tragar	trahgahr
swamp	el terreno pantanoso	ehl tehrrehnoh pahntahnohsoh

sweat	el sudor	*ehl soodohr*
sweet	el caramelo	*ehl kahrahmehloh*
sweet	dulce	*doolseh*
sweetcorn	el maíz	*ehl mahees*
sweetener	la sacarina	*lah sahkahreenah*
sweets	las golosinas	*lahs gohlohseenahs*
swim (verb)	nadar	*nahdahr*
swimming pool	la piscina/pileta	*lah peesseenah/ peelehtah*
swimming trunks	el bañador/ la malla/ el traje de baño	*ehl bahnyahdohr/ lah mahlyah/ ehl trahheh deh bahnyoh*
swindle	la estafa	*lah ehstahfah*
switch	el interruptor	*ehl eentehrrooptohr*
synagogue	la sinagoga	*lah seenahgohgah*

T

table	la mesa	*lah mehsah*
table tennis	el pingpong	*ehl peenpohn*
tablet	la tableta	*lah tahblehtah*
take (photograph)	sacar	*sahkahr*
take (time)	durar, tardar	*doorahr, tahrdahr*
take (verb)	emplear, usar, tomar	*ehmplehahr, oosahr, tohmahr*
take pictures	fotografiar, sacar fotos	*fohtohgrahfyahr, sahkahr fohtohs*
taken	ocupado	*ohkoopahdoh*
talcum powder	el talco	*ehl tahlkoh*
talk (verb)	hablar	*ahblahr*
tampons	los tampones	*lohs tahmpohnehs*
tap	la llave/canilla	*lah lyahbeh/kahneelyah*
tap water	el agua de la llave/ canilla	*ehl ahgwah deh lah lyahbeh/kahneelyah*
tart	la tarta	*lah tahrtah*
taste (verb)	probar	*prohbahr*
tax free shop	la tienda libre de impuestos	*lah tyehndah leebreh deh eempwehstohs*
taxi	el taxi	*ehl tahxee*
taxi stand	la parada de taxis	*lah pahrahdah deh tahxees*
tea	el té	*ehl teh*
teapot	la tetera	*lah tehtehrah*
teaspoon	la cuchara de té	*lah koochahrah deh teh*
telegram	el telegrama	*ehl tehlehgrahmah*
telephoto lens	el teleobjetivo	*ehl tehlehohbhehteeboh*
television	la televisión	*lah tehlehbeesyohn*
telex	el télex	*ehl tehlehx*
temperature	la temperatura	*lah tehmpehrahtoorah*
temporary filling	el empaste provisional	*ehl ehmpahsteh prohbeesyohnahl*
tender	tierno	*tyehrnoh*
tennis	el tenis	*ehl tehnees*
tennis ball	la pelota de tenis	*lah pehlohtah deh tehnees*
tennis court	la pista de tenis	*lah peestah deh tehnees*
tennis racket	la raqueta de tenis	*lah rahkehtah deh tehnees*

tennis shoes	las zapatillas de tenis	*lahs sahpahteelyahs deh tehnees*
tenpin bowling	los bolos	*lohs bohlohs*
tent	la tienda/carpa	*lah tyehndah/kahrpah*
tent peg	la estaca	*lah ehstahkah*
terrace	la terraza	*lah tehrrahsah*
terrible	terrible	*tehrreebleh*
thank (verb)	agradecer	*ahgrahdehsehr*
thank you	gracias	*grahsyahs*
thaw	deshelar	*dehsehlahr*
the day after tomorrow	pasado mañana	*pahsahdoh mahnyahnah*
theatre	el teatro	*ehl tehahtroh*
theft	el robo	*ehl rohboh*
there	allí	*ahlyee*
thermal bath	el baño termal	*ehl bahnyoh tehrmahl*
thermometer	el termómetro	*ehl tehrmohmehtroh*
thick	grueso/gordo	*grwehsoh/gohrdoh*
thief	el ladrón	*ehl lahdrohn*
thigh	el muslo	*ehl moosloh*
thin	fino, flaco	*feenoh, flahkoh*
things	las cosas	*lahs kohsahs*
think	pensar	*pehnsahr*
third	la tercera parte	*lah tehrsehrah pahrteh*
thirsty, to be	la sed	*lah sehdh*
this afternoon	esta tarde	*ehstah tahrdeh*
this evening	esta noche	*ehstah nohcheh*
this morning	esta mañana	*ehstah mahnyahnah*
thread	el hilo	*ehl eeloh*
throat	la garganta	*lah gahrgahntah*
throat lozenges	las pastillas para la garganta	*lahs pahsteelyahs pahrah lah gahrgahntah*
throw up	vomitar	*bohmeetahr*
thunderstorm	la tormenta eléctrica	*lah tohrmehntah ehlehktreekah*
Thursday	el jueves	*ehl hwehbehs*
ticket (admission)	la entrada	*lah ehntrahdah*
ticket (travel)	el boleto	*ehl bohlehtoh*
tickets	los boletos	*lohs bohlehtohs*
tidy (verb)	recoger	*rehkohehr*
tie	la corbata	*lah kohrbahtah*
tights	el panty/las medias	*ehl pahntee/ lahs mehdyahs*
time (occasion)	la vez	*lah behs*
time	el tiempo	*ehl tyehmpoh*
timetable	el horario	*ehl ohrahryoh*
tin	la lata	*lah lahtah*
tip (money)	la propina	*lah prohpeenah*
tissues	los pañuelitos de papel	*lohs pahnywehleetohs de pahpehl*
toast	el pan tostado, las tostadas	*ehl pahn tohstahdoh, lahs tohstahdahs*
tobacco	el tabaco	*ehl tahbahkoh*
toboggan	el trineo	*ehl treenehoh*
today	hoy	*ohee*
toe	el dedo del pie	*ehl dehdoh dehl pyeh*
together	juntos	*hoontohs*

toilet	el water/el baño/ el lávabo	ehl bahtehr/ehl bahnyoh ehl lahbahboh
toilet paper	el papel higiénico	ehl pahpehl eehyehneekoh
toiletries	los artículos de tocador	lohs ahrteekoolohs deh tohkahdohr
tomato	el tomate	ehl tohmahteh
tomato purée	el tomate triturado	ehl tohmahteh treetoorahdoh
tomato sauce	el ketchup	ehl kehchoop
tomorrow	mañana	mahnyahnah
tongue	la lengua	lah lehngwah
tonic water	el agua tónica	ehl agwah tohneekah
tonight	esta noche	ehstah nohcheh
too much	demasiado	dehmahsyahdoh
tools	las herramientas	lahs ehrrahmyehntahs
tooth	el diente	ehl dyehnteh
toothache	el dolor de muelas	ehl dohlohr deh mwehlahs
toothbrush	el cepillo de dientes	ehl sehpeelyoh deh dyehntehs
toothpaste	el dentífrico	ehl dehnteefreekoh
toothpick	el palillo	ehl pahleelyoh
top up	rellenar	rehlyehnahr
total	el total	ehl tohtahl
tough	duro	dooroh
tour	la excursión, el paseo	lah ehxkoorsyohn, ehl pahsehoh
tour guide	el guía	ehl geeah
tourist card	la tarjeta de turista	lah tahrhehtah deh tooreestah
tourist class	la clase turista	lah klahseh tooreestah
Tourist Information office	la oficina de (información y) turismo	lah ohfeeseenah deh (eenfohrmahsyohn ee) tooreesmoh
tourist menu	el menú turístico	ehl mehnoo tooreesteekoh
tow	remolcar	rehmohlkahr
tow cable	el cable de remolque	ehl kahbleh deh rehmohlkeh
towel	la toalla	lah tohahlyah
tower	la torre	lah tohrreh
town hall	el ayuntamiento	ehl ahyoontahmyehntoh
town/city	la ciudad	lah syoodahdh
toys	los juguetes	lohs hooguehtehs
traffic	el tráfico	ehl trahfeekoh
traffic light	el semáforo	ehl sehmahfohroh
trailer tent	el remolque tienda	ehl rehmohlkeh tyehndah
train	el tren	ehl trehn
train ticket	el boleto de tren	ehl bohlehtoh deh trehn
train timetable	la guía de trenes	lah geeah deh trehnehs
translate	traducir	trahdooseer
travel (verb)	viajar	byahhahr
travel agent	la agencia de viajes	lah ahhehnsyah deh byahhehs

travel guide	la guía	*lah geeah*
traveller	el pasajero	*ehl pahsahhehroh*
traveller's cheque	el cheque de viajero	*ehl chehkeh deh byahhehroh*
treacle/syrup	la melaza	*lah mehlahsah*
treatment	el tratamiento	*ehl trahtahmyehntoh*
triangle	el triángulo	*ehl treeahngooloh*
trim	cortar las puntas	*kohrtahr lahs poontahs*
trip	el paseo, la excursión	*ehl pahsehoh,lah ehxkoorsyohn*
trouble	la molestia	*lah mohlehstyah*
trousers (long, short)	los pantalones (cortos, largos)	*lohs pahntahlohnehs (kohrtohs,lahrgohs)*
trout	la trucha	*lah troochah*
trunk call	interurbano	*eentehroorbahnoh*
trunk code	el prefijo	*ehl prehfeehoh*
trustworthy	digno de confianza	*deegnoh deh kohnfyahnsah*
try on (clothes)	probarse	*prohbahrseh*
T-shirt	la camiseta	*lah kahmeesehtah*
tube	el tubo	*ehl tooboh*
Tuesday	el martes	*ehl mahrtehs*
tumble drier	la secadora	*lah sehkahdohrah*
tuna	el atún	*ehl ahtoon*
tunnel	el túnel	*ehl toonehl*
turn	la vez	*lah behs*
TV	la televisión	*lah tehlehbeesyohn*
tv and radio guide	la guía de radio y televisión	*lah gheeah deh rahdyoh ee tehlehbeesyohn*
tweezers	los alicates	*lohs ahleekahtehs*
tyre (bicycle)	la cubierta	*lah koobyehrtah*
tyre lever	el desmontador de neumáticos	*ehl dehsmohntahdohr deh nehoomahteekohs*
tyre pressure	la presión de los neumáticos	*lah prehsyohn deh lohs nehoomahteekohs*

U

ugly	feo	*fehoh*
umbrella	el paraguas	*ehl pahrahgwahs*
under	abajo, debajo de	*ahbahhoh, dehbahhoh deh*
underground railway	el metro/tren subterráneo	*ehl mehtroh/trehn soobtehrrahnehoh*
underground railway system	la red de metro	*lah rehdh deh mehtroh*
underground station	la estación de metro	*lah ehstahthyohn deh mehtroh*
underpants	los calzoncillos	*lohs kahlsohnseelyohs*
understand	entender	*ehntehndehr*
underwear	la ropa interior	*lah rohpah eentehryohr*
undress (verb)	desvestirse	*dehsbehsteerseh*
unemployed	sin trabajo	*seen trahbahjoh*
uneven	desigual	*dehseegwahl*
university	la universidad	*lah ooneebehrseedahd*
unleaded	sin plomo	*seen plohmoh*
urgent	urgente	*oorhehnteh*

urine	la orina	*lah ohreenah*
usually	por lo general	*pohr loh hehnehrahl*

V

vacate	desalojar	*dehsahlohhahr*
vaccinate	vacunarse	*bahkoonahrseh*
vagina	la vagina	*lah bahheenah*
vaginal infection	la infección vaginal	*lah eenfehksyohn bahheenal*
valid	válido	*bahleedoh*
valley	el valle	*ehl bahlyeh*
valuable	costoso	*kohstohsoh*
van	la furgoneta	*lah foorgohnehtah*
vanilla	la vainilla	*lah baheeneelyah*
vase	el florero	*ehl flohrehroh*
vaseline	la vaselina	*lah bahsehleenah*
veal	la carne de ternera	*lah kahrneh deh tehrnehrah*
vegetable soup	la sopa de verduras	*lah sohpah deh behrdoorahs*
vegetables	la verdura	*lah behrdoorah*
vegetarian	vegetariano	*behhehtahryahnoh*
vein	la vena	*lah vehnah*
vending machine	la máquina automática	*lah mahkeenah ahootohmahteekah*
venereal disease	la enfermedad venérea	*lah ehnfehrmehdah behnehrehah*
via	pasando por	*pahsahndoh pohr*
video recorder	el video	*ehl beedehoh*
video tape	la cinta de vídeo	*lah seentah deh beedehoh*
view	la vista	*lah beestah*
village	el pueblo	*ehl pwehbloh*
visa	la visa	*lah beesah*
visit (verb)	visitar	*beeseetahr*
visit	la visita	*lah beeseetah*
vitamin tablets	las tabletas de vitaminas	*lahs tahblehtahs deh beetahmeenahs*
vitamins	la vitamina	*lah beetahmeenah*
volcano	el volcán	*ehl bohlkahn*
volleyball (play)	jugar al vóleibol	*hoogahr ahl bohleheebohl*
vomit (verb)	vomitar	*bohmeetahr*

W

wait (verb)	esperar	*ehspehrahr*
waiter	el mesero/mozo	*ehl mehsehroh/mohsoh*
waiting room	la sala de espera	*lah sahlah deh ehspehrah*
wake up (verb)	despertar	*dehspehrtahr*
walk	el paseo	*ehl pahsehoh*
walk (take a)	salir a caminar	*sahleer ah kahmeenahr*
walk (verb)	caminar	*kahmeenahr*
wallet	la cartera	*lah kahrtehrah*
wardrobe	el guardarropa	*ehl gwahrdahrrohpah*
warm	caliente	*kahlyehnteh*
warn	avisar, llamar	*ahbeesahr, lyahmahr*

warning	el aviso	*ehl ahbeesoh*
wash (verb)	lavar	*lahbahr*
washing (dirty)	la ropa sucia	*lah rohpah soosyah*
washing line	la cuerda de colgar la ropa	*lah kwehrdah deh kohlgahr lah rohpah*
washing machine	la lavadora	*lah lahbahdohrah*
washing-powder	el detergente	*ehl dehtehrhehnteh*
wasp	la avispa	*lah ahbeespah*
watch	el reloj	*ehl rehlohh*
water	el agua	*ehl ahgwah*
water ski	el esquí acuático	*ehl ehskee ahkwahteekoh*
waterproof	impermeable	*eempehrmehahbleh*
wave-pool	la piscina con oleaje	*lah peesseenah kohn ohlehahheh*
way (means)	el remedio	*ehl rehmehdyoh*
way (on the)	en el camino	*ehn ehl kahmeenoh*
way	el lado	*ehl lahdoh*
we	nosotros	*nohsohtrohs*
weak	débil	*dehbeel*
weather	el tiempo	*ehl tyehmpoh*
weather forecast	el pronóstico del tiempo	*ehl prohnohsteekoh dehl tyehmpoh*
wedding	la boda	*lah bohdah*
Wednesday	el miércoles	*ehl myehrkohlehs*
week	la semana	*lah sehmahnah*
weekend	el fin de semana	*ehl feen deh sehmahnah*
weekend duty	la guardia de fin de semana	*lah gwahrdyah deh feen deh sehmahnah*
weekly ticket	el abono semanal	*ehl ahbohnoh sehmahnahl*
welcome	bienvenido	*byehnbehneedoh*
well	bien, bueno	*byehn, bwehnoh*
west	el oeste	*ehl ohehsteh*
wet	mojado	*mohahdoh*
wet (weather)	lluvioso	*lyoobyohsoh*
wetsuit	el traje de surf	*ehl trahheh deh soorf*
what?	¿qué?	*keh?*
wheel	la rueda	*lah rwehdah*
wheelchair	la silla de ruedas	*lah seelyah deh rwehdahs*
when?	¿cuándo?	*kwahndoh?*
where?	¿dónde?	*dohndeh?*
which?	¿cuál?	*kwahl?*
whipped cream	el chantilly	*ehl chahnteelyee*
whipping cream	la nata/crema para batir	*lah nahtah/krehmah pahrah bahteer*
white	blanco	*blahnkoh*
who?	¿quién?	*kyehn?*
wholemeal	integral	*eentehgrahl*
wholemeal bread	el pan integral	*ehl pahn eentehgrahl*
why?	¿por qué?	*pohr keh?*
wide-angle lens	el objetivo gran angular	*ehl obhehteeboh grahn ahngoolahr*
widow	la viuda	*lah byoodah*
widower	el viudo	*ehl byoodoh*

wife	la esposa	*lah ehspohsah*
wind	el viento	*ehl byehntoh*
windbreak	la protección contra el viento	*lah prohtehksyohn kohntrah ehl byehntoh*
windmill	el molino	*ehl mohleenoh*
window	la ventanilla, la ventana	*lah behntahneelyah, lah behntahnah*
windscreen wiper	el limpiaparabrisas	*ehl leempyahpahrah-breesahs*
wine	el vino	*ehl beenoh*
wine list	la carta de vinos	*lah kahrtah deh beenohs*
winter	el invierno	*ehl eenbyehrnoh*
witness	el testigo	*ehl tehsteegoh*
woman	la mujer	*lah moohehr*
wood	la madera	*lah mahdehrah*
wool	la lana	*lah lahnah*
word	la palabra	*lah pahlahbrah*
work	el trabajo	*ehl trahbahhoh*
working day	el día laborable	*ehl deeah lahbohrahbleh*
worn/used	gastado	*gahstahdoh*
worried	inquieto	*eenkyehtoh*
wound	la herida	*lah ehreedah*
wrap (verb)	envolver	*ehnbohlbehr*
wrist	la muñeca	*lah moonyehkah*
write	escribir	*ehskreebeer*
write down	anotar	*ahnohtahr*
writing pad	el bloc (cuadriculado, a rayas)	*ehl blohk(kwahdreekoo-lahdoh, ah rahyahs)*
writing paper	el papel de escribir	*ehl pahpehl deh ehskreebeer*
written	por carta	*pohr kahrtah*
wrong	mal, equivocado	*mahl, ehkeebohkahdoh*

Y

yacht	el yate	*ehl yahteh*
year	el año	*ehl anyoh*
yellow	amarillo	*ahmahreelyoh*
yes	sí	*see*
yes, please	con (mucho) gusto/ sí, por favor	*kohn (moochoh) goostoh/see, pohr fahbohr*
yesterday	ayer	*ahyehr*
yoghurt	el yogur	*ehl yohgoor*
you (formal)	usted	*oostehdh*
you too	igualmente	*eegwahlmehnteh*
youth hostel	el albergue juvenil	*ehl ahlbehrgueh hoobehneel*

Z

zip	la cremallera	*lah krehmahlyehrah*
	el cierre	*ehl syehrreh*
zoo	el parque zoológico	*ehl pahrkeh sohohlohheekoh*

Basic grammar

1 The article

Spanish nouns and adjectives are divided into 2 categories: masculine and feminine. The definite article (the) is **el** or **la**. Most masculine words end in **o** and most feminine words end in **a**.

el is used before masculine nouns, as in **el tren** (the train)
la is used before feminine nouns, as in **la playa** (the beach)
el is also used before feminine nouns beginning with the vowel **a**, as in **el agua** (water).

Other examples are:

el techo	the roof	**la casa**	the house
el hambre	hunger	**el alma**	the soul

The plural of **el** is **los**; the plural of **la** is **las**.

In the case of the indefinite article (**a, an**):

un is used before masculine nouns, as in **un libro** (a book).

una is used before feminine nouns, as in **una mesa** (a table).

The plural is constructed by adding s, as in **unos camiones** (some lorries), **unas tazas** (some cups).

Other examples are:

un padre	a father	**una madre**	a mother
un hombre	a man	**una mujer**	a woman
unos hombres	men	**unas mujeres**	women

2 The plural

The plural of Spanish nouns and adjectives ends in **s**. Examples are:

singular	plural
el avión (the plane)	**los aviones**
la manzana (the apple)	**las manzanas**

3 Personal pronouns

I	**yo**
You	**tú/Usted**
He/she/it	**él/ella**
We	**nosotros/nosotras**
You	**Ustedes**
They	**ellos/ellas**

When speaking to a person one does not know well, **Usted** is used instead of **tu** (you singular). **Usted** (sg) and **ustedes** (pl) take the third person of the verb:

e.g. **Usted sabe/Ustedes saben** you know

4 Possessive pronouns

	masculine/feminine	plural
my	**mi**	**mis**
your	**tu**	**tus**
his/her/its	**su**	**sus**
our	**nuestro/nuestra**	**nuestros/nuestras**
your	**su**	**sus**
their	**su**	**sus**

They agree with the object they modify, e.g. our house = **nuestra casa**.

5 Verbs

Note: pronouns are only used with verbs when absolutely necessary or to emphasise.

hablar	to speak
hablo	I speak
hablas	you speak
habla	he/she/you speak
hablamos	we speak
hablan	they/you speak

Here are some useful verbs:

ser	**estar** (to be)
soy	**estoy**
eres	**estás**
es	**está**
somos	**estamos**
son	**están**

Note: **estar** is used with places and also means a temporary state, e.g. **el hotel está en la plaza**, (the hotel is in the square), **la niña está cansada** (the little girl is tired).

tener (to have)	**hacer** (to do/make)
tengo	**hago**
tienes	**haces**
tiene	**hace**
tenemos	**hacemos**
tienen	**hacen**

ir (to go)	**ver** (to see)
voy	**veo**
vas	**ves**
va	**ve**
vamos	**vemos**
van	**ven**

Negatives are formed by putting no before the verb:
e.g. **no entiendo**, I do not understand; **no oigo**, I cannot hear.

6 Basic prepositions

a = to, e.g. **voy a Madrid, voy al mercado.**
en= in or at, e.g. **estoy en la tienda, estoy en casa.**